Let Me
Tell You
Something

Let Me Tell You Something

Life as a Real Housewife,

Tough-Love Mother, and

Street-Smart Businesswoman

Caroline Manzo
with Kevin Dickson

*it*books

AN IMPRINT OF HARPERCOLLINS*PUBLISHERS*

HarperCollins books may be purchased for educational, business, or sales promotional use. For information please write: Special Markets Department, Harper-Collins Publishers, 10 East 53rd Street, New York, NY 10022.

FIRST EDITION

Designed by Paula Russell Szafranski

All photos courtesy of the author except page xx © Jerritt Clark/Getty Images.

Library of Congress Cataloging-in-Publication Data is available upon request.

ISBN 978-0-06-221887-2

13   14   15   16   17   DIX/RRD   10   9   8   7   6   5   4   3   2   1

To my husband, Albert,

and my three children, Albie, Lauren, and Christopher.

It's been a long, crazy road and

although circumstances in life may change us,

we always manage to buckle up, hold on tight,

and end up home, in a house full of love, safely, together.

I dedicate this book to the four of you,

thanking you for giving me the happiest moments of my life.

Xoxoxoxo

With endless love, Caroline, Carijo, Mom, Bull Dog ;o)

In the long run, we shape our lives, and we shape ourselves. The process never ends until we die. And the choices we make are ultimately our own responsibility.

—ELEANOR ROOSEVELT

Contents

CONTENTS

Breakfast, lunch, or dinner: pick one meal a day to have with your family.

Everybody eat! Food is love.

Big families are tough, and I haven't even begun to figure them out.

There's no such thing as a perfect Christmas.

Christmas traditions evolve; embrace the changes.

Remember: it's Christmas presence, not Christmas presents.

My house is a home, not a museum. Kick your feet up and relax. If something spills, that's what mops are for.

Always serve tea in a cup with a saucer.

CONTENTS

CONTENTS

CONTENTS

PART VI: LIFE   **173**

I'm a badass with a heart; I cry at Kodak commercials.

Book smarts are great, but without street smarts and personality, you got nothing.

I laugh a lot. At myself. And so should you. Humor will get you through the hard times.

Everybody shits on a bowl. Never allow yourself to be intimidated.

Tell the truth. Lies will always bite you in the ass.

I may not be the smartest or the prettiest, but you will remember me.

You have only one life. Take that stage and own it.

I gauge my problems with one question: Will this affect my life one year from now? If the answer is yes, I solve it. If the answer is no, I don't obsess over it.

Reading will set you free.

Respect is free, but you gotta earn your keep.

I'm Albert's wife, and Albie, Christopher, and Lauren's mom, but I never forgot who Caroline Manzo is.

There's always someone out there who's got it worse than you. Say a prayer and help them.

Introduction

What am I doing here? This is probably the most frequent thought that runs through my mind these days. For the past five years I've been filming my life as part of a reality TV show, and it's been turned upside down as a result. My everyday routine is a thing of the past, and now my days can consist of anything from going to the market to going on the Jay Leno show. I never know what's about to happen, but when it does, my first thought is always, "What am I doing here?"

Over the months I worked on this book, that very thought popped into my head many, many times. I am a mother of three from suburban New Jersey. I agreed to do a TV show for one summer, just for a change from my regular routine. From the minute the show hit the air, my life changed dramatically. And now I'm writing a book?

It's been a long strange journey. I was hesitant to do the show. I wasn't interested. I had kids to raise and I had a job. Participating in a reality show was nowhere on my agenda. I auditioned for a laugh and never thought for a minute I'd get cast.

So, as you know, I did get cast and the show was a hit. There's nothing that can prepare you for something like an overnight success, and for how quickly you become public property and your privacy is left in tatters. That first year of the show was a whirlwind.

The best thing about that first season is that I resonated with viewers. People seemed to like me, and they wanted to talk to me.

The Facebook page that I'd kept to stay in touch with friends and family suddenly had more friends than Facebook permitted. I didn't even know that there was a limit on Facebook friends, but I hit that limit in no time.

What touched me most was that people would send me these incredible messages from all over the world. People wrote me that they loved my honesty, they loved my loyalty. They wanted to know how I kept my marriage so strong and how I'd raised such wonderful kids. It blew me away to have complete strangers respond to my qualities, and forgive the flaws, that I put on TV for everyone to see.

For a long time, I answered every message I received until the sheer volume became overwhelming. It went from ten messages a day to several thousand within a couple of weeks. In the beginning, I would talk to women around the world about their marital problems. I talked to gay kids in the Midwest who didn't know how to come out to their parents. I chatted to people about all kinds of life and family problems. I would try to help them as best I could, but in the back of my mind, I would always think, "What the hell am I doing here? I'm no expert, I'm just a no-bullshit woman from New Jersey who got mixed up in a TV show. What the hell do I know?"

In the five years that have passed since those crazy, early days, there's been a lot of water under the bridge. There's been a lot of drama and a lot of laughter. I've been dragged into some of the most heated catfights in reality TV history, and somehow I've been branded as a bitch or a hard-ass, which isn't fun when I consider myself to be a complete softie.

That was one of my main incentives in writing this book. I was frankly tired of being perceived as something I'm not, and I was frustrated that some people misinterpret my low tolerance for bullshit as some sort of vindictive meanness. I realized that people who watch the show don't know the real me. We shoot thousands of hours of footage just to make a sixteen-hour season. The real me—the quiet jokester who loves to read and laugh—often ends up on the cutting-room floor.

The final clincher that inspired me to write this book was the realization that I just might be able to help people. Whenever I leave the house, strangers will often come up to me and tell me that I inspired them to make a big life decision, to really reach for their own personal brass ring. I've been told that I've inspired people to leave bad relationships, to stand up for themselves, to come out to their parents, or to mend a toxic situation, among other things.

This always blows my mind. As a mother, you try to guide your children and shape them and help them grow into the best people they can be so that you can give them wings and set them free. To have complete strangers tell me that I had given them wings, that I had given them courage to fly, leaves me speechless. When I realized that for some reason, I was able to help people in this way, I felt that it was a good time for me to write this book. To know that I can be a positive influence to people, oh my God, it's amazing.

I still spend a lot of time agonizing over my "fame." I don't feel like I have accomplished anything so interesting to warrant the attention. I'm not a president, I haven't cured any diseases, and the only thing I've done is be myself on a TV show. But I agreed to start writing and see where I went.

As I wrote, I learned that we all have something to offer, regardless of our station in life, our education, or what people presume to know about us. I may not have gone to college, but I have sure lived my life. A degree in child psychology doesn't make you a mother. Holding your crying baby in your arms, or helping your teenager through a painful breakup, these are things that make you a mother.

I realized that I wanted to show people that the most important thing in life is to always be true to yourself. Always follow your heart, always act with integrity, but always be ready to take a risk, to follow an opportunity through to the end. It's OK to take a leap of faith.

Of course not everything will fall into place perfectly in your life, but there will be something in that journey that you're grateful for afterward. Sometimes the simplest decision that you make can have the most dramatic effect on your life—or someone else's.

I've lived my life by a strong but very simple moral compass. I believe in black-and-white. Even though it's a very broad-strokes way of looking at the big picture, it often helps you figure out the right—or wrong—thing to do in any situation. These were the kinds of lessons I realized that I wanted to share with others.

In this book, I'll tell you about my past and my present and the life lessons and mottos I live by—some I learned when I was young, others I picked up along the way. I'll explain as much as I can and share the life that made me the woman I am today. What I won't do is attack anybody. If you're looking for that kind of dirt, you can stop reading right now. If you look closely at the TV show, you'll see that I've never attacked anyone. I've reacted to being provoked, but even then, my goals are always honesty and aimed at reconciliation. You watch the show, so you know that I haven't always been able to arrive at peaceful resolutions with my costars, but I've always tried.

I have tried to live within my own moral code of integrity, but I'm not Mary Poppins, and I hope this book reflects that. I've never been afraid to admit that shit happens, because it does. But it's what you do when things go wrong that matters. Don't run away from your problems. Take responsibility for a mistake and learn from it. I view my life experiences, both the public ones you see on Sunday nights and the private ones I keep for my family and me, as opportunities for growth. I hope you can learn from them as well, which is why I decided to share them in the following pages.

Before we move on to the main course, I want to thank you for buying this book. I cannot believe the dreams I've been able to realize during my life, and now a huge publishing house has published this book that you're about to read. To think about it really makes me want to cry; it's so wonderful and humbling. I just want to thank you, and promise you that I will always give you the best of me, and try to make you proud of me, the way I try to make my husband and children proud. I honestly hope you like this book, that it makes you laugh, cry, and realize that you have just as much potential as I do. In five years, you could be writing the introduction to your own book, and wondering how the hell you got there! Nothing would make me happier.

Carolinisms

Here's a dictionary of all things Manzo
that will definitely help you understand what
I'm saying if we ever meet in person!

Chunkamonk—a term of endearment that Al started calling me years ago and now we call the kids chunkamonk. It means "I love you."

Bubbies—a woman's breasts

Chuckie—vagina

Peepee—penis

Cavone—a stereotypical male Italian. When you say someone is a cavone, it's not a compliment—it means they're obnoxious and loud.

Schkeeve—dirty or disgusting

Azzo—(pronounced "ah-tso") means "oh my God, are you kidding me?"

Monkey—another term of endearment

Guido—typical chain-around-the-neck musclehead kind of guy

The City—New York City

GWB—the George Washington Bridge between Jersey and New York City

Route 80—The highway that runs east/west across northern New Jersey

The Tunnel—The Lincoln Tunnel, from Hoboken to New York City

The Mall—Garden State Plaza, a mall on Route 17

The Shore—the seaside of New Jersey—Point Pleasant, Seaside Heights, Cape May, Lavallette

Route—the highway. It's a Jersey thing. We say "route" and then the highway number. Route 80. Route 46. And so on.

The diner—If you say "the diner," depending on where you are, people know exactly which diner you're talking about—if you're in Wayne, you mean Wayne Hills Diner. If you're in Clifton, you mean the Tick Tock Diner on Route 46. They're famous and everybody goes to them.

The Brownstone—my husband's function center in Paterson, New Jersey

Cafface—my daughter's makeup and tanning business in Franklin Lakes, New Jersey

BLK—my sons' line of mineral-infused water

The kids—someone's children. My mother still calls us all "the kids" when she talks about us, and I'm fifty-one.

Sunday dinner—pasta, sauce, antipas—every Sunday, we all sit down. If someone asks you to Sunday dinner, *you* know exactly what you're going to eat.

Fuhgeddaboudit—I'm over it.

PART I

PUBLIC PROPERTY

These are real, and I love my husband! I don't belong on this show!

I've said it a million times: I was perfectly happy in my life before the show came along. My life probably wasn't too different from yours; I had a routine and I was content. I woke up every day, I did the laundry, I went to the market and took care of my family. I made sure my husband's sock drawer was full and there was iced tea in the fridge. Along with my job selling real estate, that was it. I was your typical housewife.

I first heard about the show from my sister-in-law Jacqueline, who had already auditioned for it and told the producers about me. While Jacq was shooting her sizzle reel, she suggested that the producers come and film at my house. They met me and asked me to try out for the show. I thought it might be something fun to keep me occupied over the summer. Perhaps it would raise my profile as a Realtor in Franklin Lakes and help me sell a few more houses. But I was sure there was no way in hell they'd give me the job. As I listened to them describe the show, with its focus on glamour and glitz, I knew I didn't belong. The only *Housewives* show at that time was *Orange County*, and the first season of that show was relatively tame, with all these women bickering and throwing money around and getting lots of plastic surgery. I felt so boring in comparison to the women they told me they were searching for. I looked at my life, the life I love, and was certain that there was nothing special enough about it to make people want to watch it on TV.

I remember at one point during my audition, I suddenly looked at the producers, then pointed at my chest and said, "These are real, and I love my husband! I don't belong on this show!"

That's why I was shocked when they called me and said they wanted me to join the cast. They said that they saw me as a potential balance for all the other craziness they needed to make the show work. When Al got home that day, I told him the news. He and the kids were very supportive. "Do it, it's just for one summer," Al said. "Just have some fun with it."

Talk about famous last words. None of us realized the monster it would become. We never could have predicted the degree to which this "little show" would turn our lives upside down and inside out. However, it didn't take long for me to realize that I'd signed on to something that was going to explode big-time.

I watched the premiere episode of *The Real Housewives of New Jersey* in Florida—not even the full first episode, just that tiny half-hour teaser that they showed before the first season. The very next morning, I knew I'd underestimated the effect the show was going to have on my life.

The premiere was at 9:00 PM on a Monday night. We were flying home to New Jersey the next morning on a 7:00 AM flight. On the return flight, I took my seat on the plane and the flight attendant immediately came over to me and said, "I saw you on TV, I think you're sweet." Then the guy behind me chimed in, "Oh, you're that lady from TV last night, I liked your show."

This was not even twelve hours after the show hit the air. *Holy shit.* It snowballed from there. All of a sudden people wanted us to go on talk shows, to do magazine shoots, and everywhere I went, I was stopped. It just bewildered me. Overnight, people started thinking that I was a celebrity. They acted differently around me. I did not like it.

I wasn't prepared to lose my anonymity the way I did. If you Google me, you'll get a map to my house. We have drive-bys the whole weekend. People find my unlisted numbers and they call them until I change them.

Fans will also just park their car and walk right up my driveway. There's never a day that's completely private anymore. I just had to get rid of my mailbox at my house, because unsolicited visitors were leaving gifts in my mailbox, which was weird enough, and then they started stealing my mail! One day, we'll probably have to move from this house that we built and raised our kids in. It just won't be possible to live privately here. Would you like a stream of strangers banging on your door while you're trying to vacuum?

There's a common misconception that because you've watched me on the show that you know me and it's fine to come to my house and knock at the door as if we're friends, or to grab me in the street and kiss me. It's crazy. Andy Cohen explained it to me best. "Caroline, when you laugh, people laugh," he said. "When you cry, they cry. They're in your life." An actor plays a role, and the viewers don't see her in their home, there's a detachment. But I'm in their homes every single week through the show, and viewers are in mine, so that makes people feel familiar when they see me.

I've become public property, but I've also gotten amazing opportunities from the *Housewives*. I got to watch my sons' faces light up as I stood on the field at Giants Stadium. One night I was on a red carpet with Christopher and he tugged at my arm, all excited, because Adam Sandler was standing right next to us. Our family has laughed at Sandler's movies since the kids were tiny, so it was a surreal moment for us.

People give me grief for saying I'm not loving being famous. They ask me why I did the show if I'm so against fame. I get it, and if I'd had any idea that the show would be so successful, it may have prepared me for what it's done to my life. Believe me, I've tried to get used to the fame part of my job, but I'm still not completely comfortable with it. I still see myself as the old Caroline. I hate doing red carpets; I don't have a pose for those moments like a lot of the other Housewives do. I call it the Housewives stance, but I cannot master it. I've tried to get it right, but it's just not something I can do. When the other ladies pose, they look glamorous and fierce. When I try it, I just look fake and stupid. I could try harder to master it, to embrace this notion of celebrity, but that's just not me. Never will be. I still believe what I said in my first interview with producers: "I don't belong here."

Perhaps the hardest thing about moving into the public eye has

Since joining the show
I can't believe I've met . . .

Ellen Barkin: She loved my line "let me tell you something about my family," so Andy Cohen had me call her and leave it on her voice mail. She thought that was hilarious and she asked me out to dinner. We had a really nice night. She's awesome, I love her.

Rosie O'Donnell: Rosie is someone whose career I've watched and admired for so many years. For me to know her now is just crazy. I respect her tenacity with her career and her life. She's an amazing woman.

John Legend and Christy Teigen: We've become friends since our first meeting. They are a great couple, and they're adorable together.

Hugh Hefner: Hef's been a part of our lives for so long that to be talking to him in his own home was a dream come true. It was just very, very surreal and cool.

Ryan Kwanten: We spent hours together at the White House Correspondents' dinner, and it was a pleasure to find out he's the sweetest, most down-to-earth guy. I laughed all night.

been the constant assumptions about my life. I've heard them all—that my sons are gay, that my daughter's a fat pig, that my husband's in the mob. I've been called a fat, redheaded dyke. Some might say that because I put myself out there, I should deal with these insults. To hell with them! I agreed to be on a TV show, yes, but that doesn't give anyone the right to be mean or disrespectful.

BEHIND THE SCENES

The taping for the first-season reunion was disgusting. It was so cli-chéd, in a bad-movie-about-Jersey way: it was filmed in a warehouse by a rail yard, in a very industrial area. We needed to be by Jacqueline's hospital as she was about to go into labor, so they chose this random place. We suspected it was going to be a tough reunion for Jacq already, so the last thing we needed was for her to be stressed about going into labor in New York City. When I walked into that place, I was shocked at how tacky and cheesy it was—I mean, that place was falling apart. It was our first big tap-ing for the show, and it couldn't have been in a dingier place. I remember thinking, Is this what America thinks of us? Our subsequent reunion tapings, at the Borgata or wherever, are so much more glamorous, even if they're still as stressful.

I value and appreciate my fans. I will stop and talk to as many people who want to talk to me. I've gotten on the phone with more mothers, sisters, daughters, and grandparents than I can remember, just because they wanted me to talk to them because they get excited to associate with a "celebrity." But I'm still just a regular person try-ing her damnedest to make a good impression in an irregular life.

I've never been afraid to speak my mind.

I've always loved to talk, ever since I was young. When my sister Frannie watches me on TV, she tells me not a thing has changed.

Ask Caroline

Hi, Caroline! I'm a first-time mom. My daughter is nine months old, and I'm at home with her. I've recently decided to go back to school to get my master's. I'm feeling a little guilty about this, but she'll only be alone twice a week, four hours one morning, five hours one evening per week. Her dad and teenaged stepsister will watch her while I'm at school, but I just can't shake this feeling of guilt. Am I doing the right thing?

Good for you. Don't feel guilty at all. Your daughter is in good hands and won't even know you're gone. We all have the mommy guilt button, we all have it but we have to learn to shut it off every now and then.

Look at the big picture: you're doing something to better yourself, which in turn will provide better employment opportunities for you if you decide to reenter the workforce. Being a mother is the most important role in your life, but it's always important to take this time for yourself and follow your dreams.

She sees me talk to Jay Leno and Andy Cohen just how I used to talk to her when we were growing up. As one of eleven kids, I learned early on how to hold my own at the dinner table. Being part of such a huge family taught me the art of conversation, and on top of that, my father instilled in me the importance of never being afraid to speak my mind.

That's why when this show came along and we got asked to make the rounds at talk shows for promotion, I welcomed it. Talk shows have always been a piece of cake for me, even though some might say my very first appearance on a talk show was anything but a cakewalk. I was with Jacqueline and Dina on *The View,* and there was palpable tension in the air as we took the stage, in front of millions of viewers. I wasn't sure where it was coming from—until I got ambushed by all of the women of *The View!*

We were guests of the show just after Bravo had premiered the *Housewives* episode where Christopher launched his strip club/car-wash idea. Suddenly, in the middle of my first live appearance on national TV, the conversation turned to what my son had done, with the women saying it was inappropriate for a mother to allow her son to work with strippers. Even though this was happening on live television, the drama didn't faze me a bit. I just looked at them and said, *So what?*

Of course that only made things worse. They wanted me to get defensive and give them some fireworks. "What's wrong with strippers?" I continued. I just sat there and didn't get heated. I told them I supported my son and that was that. People were shocked afterward that I stood up to *The View* crew; they can be an intimidating bunch. To me, it was my only option. They'd gone after my kid, I'd defended myself. They didn't scare me, they didn't bother me. I've never been afraid to speak my mind.

Not much scares me. I'll go on any show and talk to anyone. But I'm far less comfortable doing print interviews. A bad journalist can twist your words so much that when the article comes out, you're actually saying the opposite of what you meant. It's infuriating, but it happens much more frequently than you would think. That's why I like live TV—people can see the actual words coming out of my mouth—there's no mixed messages.

BEHIND THE SCENES

Sometimes during my interview tapings I will start crying, and before you know it, the whole crew will start crying too. Guys and girls alike, all crying with me. It becomes very strange, because they have to cry in complete silence to save the shot, so you see them trying to hold back the tears. Their chins start to tremble, their eyes will fill with tears, and they struggle to keep it in check, because if they make one loud sob, the whole scene is ruined. Have you ever tried to cry silently? It's not easy. In a way, it makes me feel very supported, to be able to be so emotionally open, and have my crew, my friends, right there with me.

Plus it's a lot of fun, one of my guilty pleasures. I grew up loving talk shows, the rapport a host can have with his or her guests. My favorites are the shows that tape in front of live audiences. The energy is insane. I remember one time when I was cohosting with Regis, he told me I had been too hard on Danielle Staub. I looked at him and said, "Fine, you go spend a couple of weeks with her and tell me what you think afterward." Regis burst out laughing, and the audience followed suit. It made me feel good that I just made a roomful of people laugh—I forgot for a moment that we were on a TV show streaming live across the country. I love the spontaneity of moments like this.

I don't know what the future holds, but if the opportunity to host a talk show came along, I would do it in a heartbeat. I can think of nothing more fun than having a different group of people to meet every day. I used to dream of being a lawyer or a child psychologist, because I like talking to people and finding out about them. I'm all about joking around with people and busting their chops. It's what I do every day anyway, so whether I continue to do it on

TV or just in real life, I've got my questions prepped and I'm ready to go.

I have to pinch myself every day to make sure I'm not dreaming.

Every once in a while I get this crazy moment of clarity, like when I was sitting thirty yards away from Barack Obama at the White House Correspondents' dinner, or when I was about to walk out onto the stage of the Jay Leno show. At those moments, my brain will snap and all I can think is, "What the hell am I doing here?" I pause and say to myself, "Just go with it, Caroline, have fun." I relax and I enjoy whatever strange situation I'm in.

Never in a million years would I have imagined that my life would turn out this way. The people I've met, the things I've done—just unbelievable. I have to pinch myself back to reality. I pinch myself while we're shooting the show too. Reality TV is real. What comes out of our mouths is real, and these things happened. But if you're foolish enough to drink the Kool-Aid, and change who you are because there's a camera on you, that's when the walls will come tumbling down and you will become a puppet for the show. If you don't stay true to yourself, you're headed for trouble. No amount of money will make me say something on TV that I wouldn't say in real life.

Obviously, the show requires us to spend more time together than we normally would. There are times when we are filming that it's the last place on earth I want to be. I can sense when I'm being set up to help get sparks to fly. At those times I pinch myself, I remind myself to always keep my feet on the ground, to keep my cool until the storm passes. I know that if I walk away, the cameras catch it, and it becomes drama. But if I say anything at all, I am suddenly part of that fight.

My top five "pinch myself" moments that have happened because of the show

1. Meeting Hugh Hefner. It meant the world for me to take Al to the Playboy Mansion and then be pushy enough that he got to meet Hef.
2. Walking onstage at Jay Leno and realizing as I walked out there that I was on the Johnny Carson set. I watched Carson my whole life.
3. Attending the White House Correspondents' dinner. That was definitely a *What Am I Doing Here?* moment. And it was a lot of fun.
4. Judging the Miss USA pageant. I have watched that pageant since I was a little girl, and to think that I was part of it, even as a judge, was surreal and cool.
5. Writing this book. Books have been my salvation and my escape for my entire life. To be able to write one has been an incredible honor.

I try my best to navigate these situations—I pinch myself and it reminds me who Caroline really is—and I don't have time to waste on something so petty.

At this point, being a part of the show is a business decision, not a personal one. I've gone through too many fires on this show to quit now. But for all the grief that has come from the show's inherent drama, there have been moments where I've needed to pinch myself because things were so great. In what other life would I get to say that we were invited to the Super Bowl—my whole family—by the Mara family? We all got to sit with the owners of our hometown team, and watch them win the Super Bowl, and attend the private party afterward. Being part of that was truly a once-in-a-lifetime miracle, sharing the victory with a family of very good people who came into our lives as a result of the show. It was an incredible day.

My favorite moment of that day was looking at the faces of my husband and kids as we watched our team's victory. This was the greatest pinch-myself moment of them all. So far . . .

You wanna be on a reality show? You better toughen up.

I have always considered myself to be a survivor, but in no way was I prepared for what happened when this show hit. Getting bullets shot at you from all directions, about everything you hold dear, really tests you. Dealing with people who don't know you but think they know everything about you has been challenging and strange. But from it all I've also learned that I'm a hell of a lot stronger than I thought I was!

The most important lesson I've taken away from my time with the *Housewives* is the strength of silence. I'm sure a lot of readers have come to this book hoping that I will spill a lot of secrets or talk about my fellow cast mates. Sorry to disappoint you. Everything I need to say about the people on my show has been said on the show. There aren't any secrets or hidden information that I can share.

My trust in human nature has been shaken. Some of the Internet comments that have been written about me have been so awful, they've shocked me, and that's not easy. I quickly learned that people are cowards behind computers, armed with their anonymity they say things they'd never have the courage to say to my face. Drama sells; happiness, cookies, and cream do not. It took me a long time to realize these stories aren't personal, and that the people who read them quickly forget about them the next day. It was a lot of work for me to become OK with it, and accept it as part of my business.

Ultimately I learned that my family can get through anything. Watching the show, I am always happy to see how united we are. My kids have taken beatings on this show, and they've gotten stronger too. They've learned that the best revenge is for them to be successful in the face of someone who's calling them losers.

Fame is a drug, and it's addictive and dangerous. If you don't have your feet firmly on the ground, you're going to get destroyed. You'll be sucked into your own hype, and you will lose your way, and possibly a lot more. That will never happen to me. If my husband saw any sign of that happening to me, he would tell me, and I would quit the show in a heartbeat.

I'm very aware that I'm in the middle of my fifteen minutes. I know that if the show ended tomorrow, my Facebook friends would drop from half a million to nothing in a short amount of time. If I'm not in the public eye, people will stop caring about me pretty quickly. I know that with any fame, out of sight equals out of mind 99 percent of the time. People don't actually love me. They love what I am every week on a TV show. And they'll forget about me as fast as they loved the show when it started. I'm completely fine with this. This whole experience has been fun, and while it lasts, I'll continue to enjoy it. And when it's over, I'll go back to my life with my grace and dignity intact.

BEHIND THE SCENES

If you ever see any of us walking around Franklin Lakes without a cameraman, don't assume we're not filming! The cameras can be hidden anywhere, and people don't see them, so they rush up to tell us they love the show. What sucks is that we are filming and we can't stop to talk to them or we lose the whole scene! We literally have to ignore people, which is something I hate to do. If you've ever come running up to me and I've just kept on walking, I'm not a bitch, I was just in the middle of a scene. I feel awful every time it happens, but there's nothing else I can do . . .

This show taught me the value of staying true to myself and being real with my audience. They deserve nothing less. That's the most important thing to me. Everything you see with my name on it, it's me. I write every tweet and status update. I can't answer every message I get anymore—there are too many; it would be a full-time job. But I read them all. People who write to me are my lifeline. These people let me know when I'm doing something wrong. They keep me on the right path—not some stranger writing a gossip piece hiding behind a computer, or a bunch of bullies on Twitter or Facebook. These attacks can't hurt me. I've learned to never compromise my truth and to roll with the punches.

I've met some amazing fans . . . this one touched me the most.

One of the most heartbreaking things I've ever seen happened while I was at an event down at the Jersey Shore. I was signing autographs when a bunch of nurses came up to me. They told me about a patient that they were treating nearby.

She was suffering from seizures and depression, and had tried to take her own life after her boyfriend left her. The nurses told me that she had wanted to come to see me at this in-store appearance but she wasn't well enough, and that had made her even more depressed.

I listened to the nurses tell me this woman's devastating story, and then I asked them how far away the hospital was. When I heard it was only a couple miles, I told them that I would try to visit the woman before I headed home the following day. I didn't want them to tell anyone I was coming—least of all the patient, in case something came up and I couldn't make it. But I made them promise they wouldn't notify the press, that there'd be no photographers there. They agreed.

The next morning, I went to the hospital to visit this woman. I recognized her as soon as I walked in. She was around my age, and attractive, but you could tell she'd had a hard life. She had red hair and blue eyes. She looked up and saw me come into the room, and then tears started pouring down her face.

She didn't speak, she just sat there crying. I went to her and I told her that I'd heard she wasn't doing too well, and that I was sorry to hear that. She still didn't say anything.

I continued that I'd heard that she had also tried to hurt herself, and I asked her to talk about that with me. She and I sat for about forty-five minutes. She told me her life story—that she'd donated a kidney to her ex-husband, that she had a wonderful relationship with her sixteen-year-old son. But she had recently been dealt a bad hand. She lost her house in a foreclosure and her boyfriend had broken up with her. She told me that watching my show gave her hope that she could be as strong as me. I looked at her, and I told it to her straight.

"You just told me that you adore your sixteen-year-old son and you gave a kidney to your husband *after* you divorced him and you want to end your life just because some guy broke up with you?" I asked. I told her she was stronger than me.

I told her she was stronger than most people on this earth, and that things were going right for her. I told her that she, not me, should be out on the circuit talking to people about how to overcome difficulties in life. I told her I didn't have half the courage that she did. I told her to own the fire that came to her naturally (she's a natural redhead, mine is from the bottle). I told her that she was going to be OK and I made her promise me to have a better attitude when it came to her own safety.

Then I looked her in the eye and said, "I'm going to be honest with you. I'm never going to see you again. But I know you have the power to overcome this."

I knew she had her own strength, but she hadn't realized it yet. I hugged her and I said good-bye.

A few months later, one of the nurses called to tell me that the woman was doing really well. She'd gotten a new apartment and she'd turned her life around. I can't explain what I mean to complete strangers, but it is moments like this that make me so grateful that I can help, in a little way.

Your kid is gay? So what? He's still your kid!

Since the show started, I have absolutely loved meeting people who watch. I've loved the connection that people feel; I've loved the stories they've shared with me. Some of these encounters will stay with me for the rest of my life.

One of my favorites, which still brings tears to my eyes, was a chance meeting with a young boy last Christmas. I was out shopping by myself at Riverside Mall when a man, a typical Jersey guy, came up to me. I could tell he wanted to talk. He pointed at me, right in the chest, and told me that I was "from that show on TV" and then he lost his steam. He just stood in front of me, silently, looking at the ground.

I waited, and I noticed that he was starting to get choked up. After a while, he got himself together and looked me in the eye. "I want to thank you," he said, his voice thick with emotion.

"For what?" I asked.

"You gave me my son back," he said.

We started talking and he explained that his family watched *Housewives* and saw many similarities between my family and theirs.

The man told me the episode where Albie failed law school had changed his family focus. There was a moment in the scene when I looked at my son, told him that I loved him, and believed he could do anything.

"When my son saw that, he turned to my wife and asked her if she was just like Caroline, if she would love him no matter what he told her?" the man said.

At this point in his story, right there in the middle of Saks, this man started to cry. But he was able to continue his story. In response to her son, his wife said that yes, she was just like me and she would love him no matter what. Their son then asked if that meant he could tell them anything, and they assured him that he could.

This complete stranger then told me that this was a huge step for his family, to have his son talk to them like this. For the past year leading up to this moment, he had shut himself off from the world. He had become quiet and distracted, his grades had dropped, and his parents had lost the ability to communicate with him.

But when this kid saw me tell Albie that I'd love him no matter what, it triggered something in him, and he asked his parents if their love was unconditional. When they told him that yes it was, he looked them both in their eyes and told them that he was gay. His parents hugged and kissed him and told him that that was OK.

This guy, this complete stranger, was by now completely crying as he recounted this story to me. He said that without watching the show, without seeing me as a parent with such unconditional love, his son would not have had the confidence to come out, and he wanted to thank me. I was astounded. It was such a beautiful story that I didn't know what to say.

Then he explained to me that today happened to be his son's birthday, and that his son was at a restaurant in the mall with his mother. He asked if I would come with him and meet his family.

When we got to the restaurant, and the kid saw me standing with his dad, he literally crumbled into my arms, he was crying so hard. It was an incredible moment, I was crying my ass off. I just held his face in my hands while he cried. I kept saying "happy birthday, you're so beautiful"—I didn't know what else to say. I was a mess.

Suddenly the boy looked at his father and asked how his father had found me.

His father was crying too. "I didn't find her, she found us," he said.

It's moments like this, moments of pure, real emotion and healing, for people I don't even know, that make everything else about doing this show completely worth it.

Loyalty is important, but it's a two-way street.

There's something I want to get straight with you. You've seen me deal with a lot of complex emotional situations over the past four years. From the mail I get, it seems that a lot of viewers are confused by my words and my actions. People write me and say I always talk about loyalty, but I haven't shown loyalty to my fellow cast mates. I consider myself loyal to a fault, but that doesn't mean I'm an idiot.

Loyalty means always telling the truth, even if someone doesn't want to hear it. And sometimes, your loyalty demands that you walk away from somebody rather than turn on them or be a fake friend.

First and foremost, I am loyal to myself. I cannot fake it with anyone. There's no way on earth I can sit at a table with a person I don't like and not let it show. I find it impossible to look at someone who's doing something horribly, drastically wrong and say "that's OK" when it's not. I just can't. Maybe if I could, things would be easier.

I think it's been proven that I prefer to stay quiet on the show. I have avoided as many confrontations as I can. I have tried so hard

Ask Caroline

Hey Caroline! I'm a twenty-four-year-old college guy who is gay, but I haven't told my mom yet. If you were my mother, how would you want your son to come out to you?

I'm going to assume that your relationship with your mom is healthy. I understand that there's a level of discomfort in discussing your sex life with your mother, and you might be worried that your mom may not understand or could condemn your sexuality.

Let me tell you this: I'd be surprised if she doesn't have a good idea that you're gay already. A mother's instinct is intense. She's probably just waiting for you to bring it up.

Wait for a time when you have her undivided attention so you can talk in private, without interruption. Speak from your heart, and be open and honest. Help her understand the emotions you've been dealing with on your journey, and show her what it feels like to be you.

If your mom is in fact shocked by your admission, just give her the time she needs to absorb things and then revisit with her.

As a parent, the one thing I want is for my children to live a life full of health, peace, and happiness. Everything else is unimportant. There's nothing worse than a parent watching their child suffer. I imagine that this secret from your mom is standing in the way of you living your life in peace and being happy. Good luck, and no matter what your mom's reaction is, I want you to be proud of who you are. I wish you all the happiness life has to offer you.

to never add any fuel to the fights or feuds that happen around me. And somehow I have gained a reputation for being forceful. I don't understand it.

I can count on one hand the times I've stooped to confrontation on the show: I lost my temper during the first-season finale, when Danielle started attacking my family. I hated myself for getting sucked into it, but out of loyalty to myself and my family, I had to speak up. The second time was when I agreed to meet with Danielle in season two. At that meeting, as tensions rose, I called her a clown. To this day, even though "clown" is hardly the worst thing you could call someone, I regret that choice of words. I don't like to hurt people but I'm not a coward. If something needs to be addressed, I prefer to do it without name-calling. Danielle pushed and pushed at that meeting and I called her a clown, and it hurt her. I felt horrible.

BEHIND THE SCENES

We have to be constantly aware of continuity while we're filming—if we start filming a scene, we have to finish it; it's not like we can just get up and disappear in the middle of a scene. When we were in Punta Cana, I got one of the worst migraines I'd ever had. I wanted to crawl into a hole and die. But we'd been filming, so they had to incorporate my migraine into the story, and then they insisted that I drag myself out of bed to watch Teresa try on bathing suits for forty-five minutes, but I could barely see. Watch that scene again—you can tell how sick I am. When I was allowed to go back to my room, I curled up on the bathroom floor with ice packs on my head, and threw up for the entire day while everyone else was out having fun.

The third confrontation was this past season on the show. I was forced into confrontations by Teresa over what she wrote about me in her book. This is the *first* time anyone has seen me gun for Teresa, but I was actually done with her in season two. We were not friends before the show started, so I didn't see any point to try to salvage a relationship that I never had. We're not friends, we're not enemies, we're cast mates. How do you feel about everyone at your work? Some people you want to hang out with, some people you don't want to hang out with. That's how it is on our show. Sometimes, we're just together for work.

Whatever I've gone through with this show, and whatever the future seasons have in store for me, I know that my kids and my grandkids will always be able to watch the show and see me doing the right thing.

You have to understand that on our television show, we shoot thousands and thousands of hours of tape. This gets boiled down to forty-five-minute episodes, and each of the five or six women has a story line. Only a fraction of what they film makes it onto the air. A five-hour event makes for a two-minute segment of the show. The camera doesn't lie, but quite often my motivation ends up on the cutting-room floor. We've had scenes that were so funny that the cameramen dropped their cameras they were laughing so hard. But those scenes aren't what the public wants to see. I wish people wanted to watch us getting along and having fun, but viewers are much more likely to tune in to a train wreck.

I sometimes miss the way things were during the first season of the show, when it was all laughing and talk of "bubbies." Almost every scene we shot was amusing to us. I miss the fun of the first season. These days, in many scenes, you can tell by my body language that I don't want to be sitting in the middle of that bullshit. My shoulders are slumped and I've got a real puss on my face. You didn't see that look on my face during the first season.

But let's face it—our show wouldn't have ever grown into what it became if we hadn't discovered that scandal about Danielle Staub in season one. Had Teresa not flipped that table, we would never have been as big as we are. That whole drama ultimately set the benchmark

The top five *Real Housewives* of *New Jersey* feuds

1. Teresa v. me over what she said in her cookbook. You all know how that ended up.
2. Danielle v. Teresa at the season-two reunion. That was really unpleasant and intense.
3. Danielle v. me at the season-one reunion. That was legendary, but I couldn't tolerate what she was doing to my sister.
4. Jacqueline not turning up to the season-three reunion because of Teresa's behavior. It was awful to watch Jacqueline so distraught.
5. Teresa v. everyone in season four. We all wanted her to be accountable for what she told the press.

for the series, and that makes me sad, because in the season leading up to that, we had fun. The show was almost a comedy at times. And these days I think the show could be so much more; it could be life lessons sprinkled with good humor and heartbreak.

I went through some stinging betrayals on this show. They were devastating to go through in my life and it was devastating to watch them on TV. *Housewives* is not scripted, it's not set up. The things you watch on TV actually happened in my real life and I have to deal with them long after the cameras stop rolling.

It's not that I don't like being on the show. It's just that there are parts that are very hard at times. But I am loyal to the show, I signed up for it, and I honor my commitments. Loyalty is important to me. It means the world to me that your loyalty to my TV show has brought you to my book, and you've read this far. When I hear from a viewer that I've helped her in a positive way, it lets me know that being loyal to myself is the most important thing I can do.

The top ten signs it's time to break up with a friend

1. When you lose trust in that person, and your gut reacts differently to them.
2. When you see that there is a change in their behavioral pattern that you're not comfortable with.
3. When the negatives outweigh the positives.
4. When you're arguing more than agreeing with them.
5. When you find yourself not thinking of that person when something good happens and you want to share it—that person's not even on your radar.
6. When you need to talk, they're not the one you think of.
7. When you're not comfortable in their presence.
8. When communication breaks down on either side.
9. When you try to converse and there's no common ground.
10. When you hear that they are bitching about you behind your back.

BEHIND THE SCENES

In the early days, we'd all bring our jewelry to the reunion-show taping and other public tapings. We'd share our jewelry with one another in the green room. It was fun and it helped break the tension before we went onto the set. In the first-season reunion, Teresa is wearing my necklace. Jacqueline and I still do this, but we have so many newcomers in the cast, we just don't share as much. I still bring extra jewelry in case one of them needs it. Better to be safe than sorry!

PART II

TRADITIONS

Breakfast, lunch, or dinner: pick one meal a day to have with your family.

It's so important to have a meal with your family every day. That's the time you reconnect. Put your BlackBerry down, put your iPad down, and give your family your undivided attention.

I know we're all busy these days, so I'm not talking about a formal sit-down dinner at the table. You can eat around the kitchen island, you can stand or you can sit, you can even go to McDonald's. The main thing is that at least one meal a day isn't rushed, or eaten on the go. You take the time out of your day and you connect with whoever is around. It's about a shared experience that's fun and pleasurable for everyone.

Al worked so much that he was never home for dinner with us. There was a time when for a few months he would try to make it home early, but it just made his day crazier. So the solution was for me to take the kids down to The Brownstone and we'd eat dinner at his desk. A couple times, we had Easter Sunday dinner with the kids at his desk.

It doesn't matter where you eat, as long as you're together.

It also doesn't matter what you eat. You can serve a peanut butter sandwich and still have a great conversation. The best meal that I made for the kids was also the simplest: star soup and a grilled cheese sandwich. Star Soup is so easy—it's chicken broth with pastina in it. Salt, pepper, cheese. You serve it with grilled cheese on toast or on English muffins. The whole meal for the three kids probably cost under seven dollars and takes five minutes to make. And it's still one of their favorite dishes. Whenever Christopher comes over, one of the first things he'll say will be "Mom, Star Soup?" Even if it's one in the morning, he'll ask and I'll make it. It's a great-stick-to-your-ribs meal, and kids love it.

Our family always prioritized these family dinners. Even with

Star Soup

This is so simple, but one of my kids'
all-time favorites to this very day!

½ lb. "pastina" pasta, cooked and drained
1 can College Inn chicken broth (14½ oz.)
Salt and pepper, to taste
Grated cheese (optional)

Return the cooked, drained pasta to the pot
and add the broth, salt, and pepper, and heat to
desired temperature. DONE! I told you it was easy!

Albie is a grated cheese addict, so he always
adds cheese to his soup; Lauren and Christopher
are fine with it as is!

SERVES ABOUT 3 (HOW CONVENIENT!)

the challenges of Al's demanding job. But now, after thirty years of marriage, I can tell you that these meals became the glue that held us together and kept us connected.

If your husband is a workaholic who's never home, or if you're the one with the crazy schedule, you're going to find the family meal difficult at first. Be prepared to eat whenever you can—if it's breakfast at 5:00 AM or dinner at 3:00 AM, it can be done. Being tired all day is a small price to pay for showing someone you love them, and getting to hear about what's going on in their life.

I know that life is speeding up for all of us. We're bombarded from the minute we wake up—from our families, our friends, the TV, and all the social media we didn't even dream of ten years ago. That's why it's more necessary than ever to drop out of that madness completely, just for a half hour, once a day. You'll learn more important stuff in that half hour with your kid or husband than if you spent the whole day on Facebook.

Ask Caroline

Caroline, my husband and I have grown apart over the years and have definitely become less intimate since the birth of our daughter a year ago. He's struggling to find his feet and get a job while I'm running the house. I do feel like my love for him has lost some of its passion and we're trudging along. We're under a lot of stress. Can you tell us how to find each other again and bring back the passion?

Don't get discouraged. You and your husband have a lot on your plate. Navigating your way through new parenthood is hard enough, but you guys have financial problems hanging over your heads. Realize that you have to work as a team. There's no room for the blame game here. Be grateful for your daughter, and as long as your husband is actively looking for work, you need to remain positive and supportive. It's not unusual to feel disconnected right now, your roles have changed from partners to parents and you need to adapt.

Make an effort to reconnect with your husband. Spend time together without discussing the pressures of your life. You don't need to do grand gestures, just give your undivided attention to each other, hold hands, laugh and enjoy the simplicity of moments you share together. Believe me, a little bit of love and attention goes a long way. Marriage can be backbreaking work, but anything worth keeping usually is.

Everybody eat! Food is love.

In my life, everything revolves around food. Whether somebody is born or has just died, gotten engaged or divorced, the first thing I think is, "Want me to bring food over?"

If somebody is upset, I'll make them cookies. If it's cold outside, I'll make soup.

Now that the kids are out of the house, I don't cook as much as I used to. The boys aren't home anymore, and Lauren has the store, so there's no point. I've cooked enough in my life for a growing family that these days I don't feel like cooking for myself when

My all-time favorite meals

Sunday dinner: It's the great constant in my life to know that every Sunday, my house will be full of people I love, talking and laughing. It's all about family and friendship and is incredibly important to me.

Christmas Eve: This is my hugest holiday meal and it's my favorite. I look forward to it all year.

Breakfast with Al every day: Before Al goes off to work we either eat together at home or go out and grab breakfast. We connect and chat, and it starts the day off perfectly.

One meal a day with at least one of my kids: I make it a mission to have a meal with at least one of my kids every day. It's fun and casual, and I cherish it.

Birthday dinners: Any birthday dinner is a great fun meal in my family. The five of us always go somewhere together to celebrate.

it's just me. I'm not sad about the change. Lauren and I still cook together when she's home, and I still have to cook for enough family events, so I continue to do my time in the kitchen. And I love it. It's one of the most satisfying things in my life, to be able to cook something special for the people I love and then watch them enjoy it.

I cook every Sunday at home, and now when I go to visit the boys in Hoboken, Christopher loves to cook for me. When he's cooking, he always texts me pictures of whatever he's making or he'll call me and ask for a recipe and I'll talk him through it. He has inherited my love of cooking, and that makes me so happy.

Food is one of the best ways for me to connect with my family and my past. Think about it—you're sitting in your kitchen and you smell something cooking; you close your eyes, and suddenly, you're twelve again. The smells can take you back to wonderful places. I can be transported to my mother's kitchen in my childhood by the smells of Thanksgiving dinner cooking in the oven. The smells that I remember from my grandmother's kitchen are going to be the same smells that my grandchildren grow up with.

Food is tradition, food is love. Nothing is better for bringing a bunch of strangers together than a nice home-cooked meal and a cocktail.

Listen, I'm not saying you have to slave over a stove for hours every day. If you're busy and you need to heat up frozen dinners for your kids, that's your prerogative. Just make it special. If you're microwaving a store-bought meal for your kids, involve them in it. Let them poke the holes in the plastic, serve it to them on a funny plate. Always approach food in ways that shows your kids that you care.

BEHIND THE SCENES

I treat my crew like guests in my home. I tell them to pretend they live there too. They don't have Porta Potties, they use my bathrooms. They're welcome to help themselves to the fridge. We don't have catering, but they're all so self-sufficient, they always bring stuff to eat even when I've told them it's not necessary. If I'm cooking, I'll cook for them. If I order pizza, I order for them. It's starting to sink in—finally, they've stopped asking if they can get a cookie, and they're all helping themselves to my leftovers. I wouldn't have it any other way—these people work so hard, we could never do the show without them and they don't get enough credit.

When Albie was young, I would make him a sandwich that he loved. He called it a Specialty. It was just three slices of white bread with peanut butter spread in between. He would come home from school and say, *Mom, please make me a Specialty.* And then when he was nine or ten, he decided that he would make Specialties for everyone. Even now, at twenty-six years of age, if I offered Albie a Specialty, he'd say, *Oh my God, yeah!* This sandwich is one of the easiest meals you can make, but because we named it and treated it like something more special than it was, it has become a family food tradition with my kids.

I get a lot of mail from women who say they don't know how to cook, or they just can't cook.

My Signature Recipes

Every person should have their own signature gravy or sauce that they develop over the years. It should be custom-tailored to your taste, and you should guard the recipe. I love making my sauce, and while I change it up from time to time, here's the basic recipe—use this as a springboard to create your own personalized sauce!

Sunday Gravy

Olive oil for browning meat (about 4 to 5 tablespoons)
8 cloves garlic, crushed
1 small onion, chopped
2 pounds Italian sausage (I use 1 pound sweet, 1 pound hot)
3 veal neck bones
3 pork bones (ribs are fine)
1 beef braciole (recipe below)
3 28-oz. cans crushed or whole tomatoes
2 6-oz. cans tomato paste
1½ cups red wine
Handful of fresh basil leaves or 3 bay leaves (your choice)
Salt and pepper

In a large pot simmer the olive oil over medium heat. Add the garlic and onion and sauté for about a minute, but don't let it burn! Add the sausage, bones, and braciole. Let meat simmer for a bit and turn until all sides are browned, about 5 minutes.

Add the tomatoes along with the tomato paste to the pot and simmer for about 10 to15 minutes; we want to blend all the flavors. Once the sauce begins to bubble a bit, turn down the heat and add the wine.

Add the basil/bay leaves, and salt and pepper, to taste, keeping the pot on low heat, stirring occasionally. We don't want the sauce to stick to the pot and burn. Let the sauce simmer for about 2½ hours.

Though I throw some meatballs in midway so they absorb all the flavors of the gravy, I do keep a

(continued)

fair number out too, since Al and the kids like them fried without sauce.

Once the sauce is done, remove from the heat and discard the bones. Serve over pasta of your choice. Get yourself some good grated cheese and Italian bread and enjoy!

Braciole

Lean beef slices—buy one flank steak and slice it into thin pieces
1 cup grated Locatelli Pecorino-Romano or Parmesan cheese
Salt and pepper, to taste
5 cloves garlic, minced
½ cup fresh chopped parsley

Lay the beef slices out on a cutting board. Sprinkle with the grated cheese, salt and pepper, garlic, and parsley.

Roll up each beef slice and secure with string or toothpick to create a bunch of little beef roll-ups.

I say *bullshit*. Everyone can cook one thing well; you just haven't figured it out yet. Think about your favorite dish that your mom made for you. I bet it wasn't anything fancy. It was probably her spaghetti or her cupcakes or cookies. It might have even been something frozen that she heated and served her own way. You don't have to be a chef to make your family some food that they love. Trust me, they will love you for making even something very simple for them. It's the process of cooking, putting love and care into it, as much as the end result, that draws us closer to our families.

Ask Caroline

Caroline! Help! My mother-in-law can't cook, and it's our tradition that we always spend Thanksgiving at her house. Nobody eats their food, it's so awful. I tried talking to my husband about having it at our house, or even for us to arrive early so I can help her cook, and my husband said no! My husband says Thanksgiving isn't all about the food, but I don't think I can do this every year. How can I bring up her bad cooking without causing conflict with my husband?

Sorry, I'm with your husband. Your mother-in-law can't cook? So what? It's just one day a year, and it's clearly important to her, and to your husband. The holidays are about so much more than the food.

However, if you have a good relationship with his mom, you could offer to get there early and help, and make it seem like something fun that you'd like to do with her. You could also offer to bring some dishes with you as additions to the meal. But if any of these suggestions cause insult or hurt to your mother-in-law, drop them immediately.

Bottom line is this: it's only one day a year. It's not going to kill you. Look at the bigger picture and deal with it.

Big families are tough, and I haven't even begun to figure them out.

My family is insane, and I love it. Today we are eleven middle-aged adults with lives of our own, but in many ways, we are still the same kids we always were, and things are still as complex and strange as ever.

I marvel at how each one of us has had such a unique experience growing up in the very same household. It's amazing how differently we perceive our childhoods. There were eleven kids in one house, but if you talk to each of us, you'll get eleven different versions of our upbringing. Quite often, when we get together and start reminiscing, it won't be long before we get to bickering! "Are you nuts?" someone will say. "That's not how it was!"

My parents were very strict and we had to do our own work around the house. The brothers had to take care of the outside of the house—painting, yard work, construction—and the girls had to take care of the inside. And one of my sisters talks about it as if we were slaves. If you ask me or some other sisters, we remember it as fun, that we enjoyed all hanging out and doing our chores together. When I was sixteen, we moved to a gorgeous mansion on a lake with thirty-five rooms. We grew up in an 18,000-square-foot home with an amazing pool. We lived a very nice life and were in no way servants. But as I've learned, that's just my view of things, and that doesn't make it the absolute truth!

I look at my own three kids, who were raised in the same house with the same parents. Their values are the same, but they're completely unique people. That's what I learned from being in a big family: that you'll share core beliefs, but everyone is an individual. I'm thankful for that lesson. From a young age I became accustomed to accepting different opinions and different behaviors, and it's a skill that has served me well throughout my life. My siblings range

Ask Caroline

Caroline, as a member of a huge family I need your help! I'm visiting my boyfriend's family for the first time. He is one of ten kids, ranging from twelve to twenty-eight years old. My mother taught me to never turn up empty-handed, but how do I bring something that appeals to everyone? And do I bring a separate hostess gift for the mother? Help!

I agree with your mom, but you're taking it to an unnecessary level. You are in no way obligated to bring gifts for the whole family, and I'd be willing to bet that nobody expects you to.

A bouquet of flowers, a favorite cake or cookies, or something thoughtful like that are more than adequate as a hostess gift. Anything more than that will likely make your boyfriend and his family uncomfortable.

nineteen years in age, from forty to fifty-nine. So many different thoughts and perspectives in the same house.

It was never calm in our house. You'd have a war with one sister and another would become your ally. The next week, the roles would reverse. It kept me nimble, and it really taught me never to hold a grudge with family. I learned the skills of negotiating, of fighting right and of making peace. I had to find my way through complex shit every day, and it made me who I am.

The family dynamic was always evolving and changing—at first my sisters were my best friends and my brothers were my protectors, later on my brothers became my friends as my sisters went off and got friends their own age—but even with the changes somehow it also always stayed the same. We were the Lauritas, and that was that. Our family made sense to us, and that was all that mattered.

Once my siblings started to marry and we had to add brothers- and sisters-in-law, and then nieces and nephews, it became even more complex. They all fell into the same routines, the cliques just got bigger, and the dynamic got more complicated, but it's wonderful and has been a true blessing.

Ask Caroline

Hi Caroline, I have a troublesome relationship with my sister. We are very different people, with little in common. I feel pressured from other family members to be close to her and come to her aid whenever required, at the cost of any situation I may be experiencing. Is it selfish to want to cut ties in an attempt at self-preservation?

I'm sure you've heard the saying "You can choose your friends, but you can't choose your family." We live in a society that suggests that we should automatically get along and live a fairy-tale existence within the family dynamic. That couldn't be further from the truth. The simple fact is although you may be related by blood, it doesn't necessarily mean your personalities will blend—after all, we're only human. You have the right to your feelings, and a relationship between two people should never be expected or demanded by anyone.

(continued)

Although you may not have anything in common with your sister, I'm sure you love her, and if push came to shove and she really needed you, I imagine you'd be there for her. Having said that, it doesn't mean you need to be her doormat. As an adult you get to choose the people you have relationships with and spend time with.

I'm sure there is a fair amount of guilt regarding your parents and extended family members, but if you have tried to overcome any issues you have with your sister and you just don't click, then stop beating yourself up, get over the guilt. We live in a fast-paced world, so use your time and emotions effectively. Don't overthink things and bring undue stress upon the situation.

When you are with your sister. be civil, have a conversation, and show respect. Take one day at a time and have no greater expectations than getting through each meeting without confrontation.

Bottom line is you need to be *you* and live your life in a way that suits you. As long as you are not adding wood to the fire, your parents should respect your decision to live your life free of stress.

For all of the ups and downs of a large family, I wouldn't trade it for the world. To be fifty-one and have all ten siblings and both parents alive and healthy, all talking to each other and with a deep bond between us, makes me the luckiest person on earth. Just don't ask my siblings—you'll get a completely different story!

> ## Never compare the kids
>
> One lesson I took from growing up with so many sib-
> lings that I have applied to my own parenting is to never
> compare my kids to each other. The worst thing I ever
> heard when I was little was, *Why can't you be more like
> your sister?* It's a horrible thing to say to a kid who's
> trying to establish her own identity.

There's no such thing as a perfect Christmas.

Every year when Christmas rolls around the madness begins, *crap, I have so much to do, I have to fight the crowds, I have to buy the food, I have to buy the presents, I have to wrap the presents, I have to decorate the house.* But I see all of this as part of the fun and find ways to make every aspect of the holidays enjoyable. I wouldn't trade the insanity for the world (then again, maybe I'm a little crazy). My love for that one holiday blinds me to the stress of it. I think of Christmas the way I think of childbirth—it's insanely stressful and painful, but the minute the hard part is over, you forget it immediately and it was all worth it.

I fall for the Christmas stress trap every year in a big, bad way. It's stress piled on top of anxiety and pressure, and I'm just as guilty as the next person of leaving things to the last minute and rushing back and forth to the mall, supermarket, and Internet. The work is always the same and it's always a lot, but it's my frame of mind that gets me through it. I know the happiness this will bring to my children and that Christmas only happens one day a year. For me it's worth it. It's chaos and it drives me absolutely crazy, but through it all, I know one thing: my table will be set beautifully, there'll be a gorgeous centerpiece on it, and at the end of it all, there'll be a wonderful gathering of my family and friends.

BEHIND THE SCENES

When we agreed to let the cameras film our Christmas for season three, it just didn't occur to me that we'd be forcing our crews to miss their own Christmas as a result. I felt horrible when I realized the crew would be spending Christmas at my house, not with their own families. So what you didn't see is that we set a complete second table in the dining room for the crew so they got to sit and have Christmas dinner with us. Lauren and I also went and got every crew person a personalized gift, and we gave each of them a gift bag with my homemade hot chocolate mix, a mug, and some hats, socks, and gloves, because they freeze when we film in the winter.

Sure, there'll be drama, there'll be stuff going wrong, but let me tell you this: Christmas is still my favorite holiday. Hands down.

We have a pregame on Christmas eve. If there's fifty people coming here on Christmas Day, we do everything the night before Christmas eve. So on the night of the twenty-third, we drop everything and get into the kitchen and do all the baking. It's one of my favorite nights of the year. I don't want to bake a week before and freeze it; I like to do it on the twenty-third. And every year, all my sisters, all my sisters-in-law and nieces, they all come here and we cook. My mom comes too.

The guys hang out, playing video games and shooting the shit, and all the girls are in the kitchen, baking. Every now and then a guy will wander in and help chop and they'll stay and laugh. We're up until three o'clock in the morning, and it doesn't feel like a chore at all. It feels like family.

On the twenty-fourth I'm tired and there's so much to do. I have to set the entire table and get the whole house ready. The phone never stops ringing, this person isn't coming, that person is having some other drama, this other person is on a diet and wants diet food. I just listen, make mental notes, and keep on getting the house ready.

There's no such thing as a perfect Christmas. Someone's late, someone's not gonna come, someone's drunk. Something always happens, and that's just part of it. No point in getting cranky about it or letting it get to me. On Christmas Day, if someone wants to be an asshole, they can be an asshole. If people want to fight, that's fine, they can fight as long as they let me eat. You need to accept that a perfect Christmas will most likely involve some sort of drama. Instead of letting it "spoil the day," just roll with it.

We had a Christmas a few years ago that was definitely one of the worst. My mother decided she was going to leave my father, right before Christmas. Did I mention that she was seventy-one years of age? She decided she wanted to change her life up a bit. She came to stay at my house, so my father didn't come to Christmas that year. That was not a good year. And thankfully she changed her mind.

This past Christmas was the opposite. I had a house full of people, laughing and loving. We had complete chaos, of course, there weren't enough chairs, Lauren was yelling at Albie and Chris to get more chairs, people were sitting all over the place. The table barely got set, kids were running around, adults were falling asleep, the house was completely trashed, but I was perfectly, serenely happy. That's Christmas to me.

If Christmas truly feels like a chore to you, rein it in a little bit. Make it less of a production, but keep it personal. It's not about the money you spend, it's about the time you spend. Whether you nearly kill yourself like I do, or you take it easy and have a lovely

How to set the perfect table, Caroline-style

I love to set a table, but there's nothing more boring than a perfectly matched and set table. Setting a table should be about you and your personality and the holiday at hand. It's something to have fun with, not something to try to get perfect.

1. Start with your tablecloth and napkins. Nice linen sets are perfect for most table settings, but if you're doing BBQ, go ahead and use a plastic one for an informal yet still themed setting.

2. I love holiday table decorating. For Easter, it's all potted plants and ceramic rabbits and pastel dinnerware. For Christmas, it's a garland and candles and poinsettias, and lots of reds and greens and golds. Most days, if you stopped by my place for a meal, you'd get paper napkins and maybe even plastic cups. I don't go crazy every day . . .

3. A beautiful table has a cloth and a runner, but they don't have to be a matching set, and I also don't care if the dinnerware matches. Sometimes I'll mix and match for the same themed meal. I like to make it fun. I like using napkin rings, but sometimes I'll tie a ribbon bow around the linen napkin instead.

4. I like to set out three glasses—wine, water, and goblet, but it depends on what you're serving. I also mix and match the glasses. You want people to see the table and think of your taste, your style, not that you went and bought a whole packaged deal at a store.

> 5. A perfect table setting doesn't have to cost an arm and a leg. I always shop at stores like Marshalls and Home Goods to find interesting pieces.

low-key day with your family, what matters most is that your family is together, happy, and healthy. Nothing can beat that.

Christmas traditions evolve; embrace the changes.

My love of Christmas began when I was a kid. Christmases were always unbelievable. My father's plastics company provided plastic to the major toy makers, Ideal, Mattel, you name it. So come Christmas, we'd get a massive truckload of toys delivered from the toy companies! More toys than we could even dream of playing with.

As I transitioned to being a parent myself, I wanted Christmas to be just as special. I have always remembered and cherished the feeling of how special my parents made Christmas for me and my siblings, and that is what I've brought in my role as mother to my own children.

The number of people in the house doesn't matter, the number of presents under the tree doesn't matter either. As long as you've got a house full of love and laughter, your Christmas will be perfect.

Being from a big family means that there's always a lot of juggling when it comes to the holidays. Today things have changed, but all eleven of my siblings are a part of each other's holiday celebrations, and we include our parents, and we also have our own kids. As you can imagine, it can get hectic. In recent years, Jacqueline and I have started trading off and hosting most of the holidays. I'll do Christmas, she'll do Thanksgiving. One of us will take Easter and one of us will take a big birthday. My brother Chris is as fond of the family traditions as I am, so that's why we share.

At this point in my life the hosting traditions are shifting. The younger generation wants to do the cooking, and soon they'll want to start hosting. Lauren and my nieces are already taking over in the kitchen, and they're learning the family recipes. Teaching my daughter and nieces the secrets to recipes I learned from my mother has been incredibly touching. I actually can't wait until the first one of them asks to host Christmas, I don't even care if it's Lauren or one of my nieces. I know I'm just going to be so proud.

Since I started on the show, I've been so busy in the lead-up to Christmas that I just haven't had enough time to do everything. Rather than let traditions lapse, my kids have all stepped up to make sure that they continue.

RECIPES

Nutella Pizza

1 lb. pizza dough (you can make your own, but you can cut the prep time in half by buying fresh pizza dough from the refrigerator section of your local supermarket or pizzeria)

¼ cup flour for prepping the dough

¼ cup melted butter

1 jar chocolate-hazelnut spread, I prefer the Nutella brand. You don't have to use the entire jar, but it's good to spread it on thick.

(continued)

2 cups fresh fruit of choice—I generally use sliced
   bananas, sliced strawberries, halved raspberries,
   and blueberries
1 sprig fresh mint, to taste, for garnish (optional)
Confectioners' sugar, for garnish
Raspberry sauce, to taste (optional, you can purchase
   raspberry sauce at your local supermarket or see my
   recipe below)

Heat oven to 450°F.

Line a heavy large baking sheet with parchment paper. Lightly dust the pizza dough with the flour and roll out onto the prepared baking sheet. Make little indentations in the dough by working it with your fingers. Brush the dough with the melted butter, then bake until the crust is a light golden brown, about 20 minutes.

Remove the pizza from the oven and spread desired amount of hazelnut spread onto crust. Don't go crazy, a nice even layer is enough, you don't want it too thick!

Slice the bananas and strawberries and spread them evenly over pie. Add other berries as desired.

You can add a couple of sprigs of fresh mint if you'd like, if not, no big deal.

To finish it off you can either sprinkle a little confectioners' sugar on top or drizzle a fruit glaze. My favorite is raspberry; again, don't go crazy, just a light drizzle.

Fruit Glaze

Below is an easy recipe for a raspberry glaze, but if you're not in the mood to make it from scratch, you can find tons of different glazes in your local market.

2 cups raspberries, fresh or frozen
2 Tbsp. fresh lemon juice
6 Tbsp. sugar

Puree the berries in a blender with the lemon juice. Slowly add the sugar until blended. Strain through a fine strainer, pressing with a rubber spatula to release the juices and eliminate seeds.

Spaghetti Aglio e Olio

This is my boys' favorite dish. It's so simple, but it's really delicious. You can feed a family of five for under ten dollars!

1 lb. spaghettini or angel hair pasta, cooked and drained
½ cup olive oil
4–5 large cloves garlic, smashed, not chopped
¼ cup minced parsley
3 Tbsp. chicken stock
½ cup grated Locatelli Pecorino-Romano cheese (or fresh Parmesan)
Hot pepper flakes to taste

(continued)

Cook the pasta according to the directions on the package. Drain.

Heat the oil in a skillet, over medium heat. Add the garlic and sauté gently until it starts to brown. Remove the skillet from the heat immediately.

Pour the olive oil and garlic over the pasta. Add the parsley and chicken stock. Toss and serve immediately.

Top with the cheese and pepper flakes to taste.

SERVES 4.

Pork Chops, Potatoes, and Vinegar Peppers

Our traditional Sunday dinner always has a main course after the pasta. Here is a recipe for Christopher's absolute favorite dish that I cook.

8 medium-size Yukon Gold potatoes, washed, peeled, and cubed
4–6 center-cut 1-inch-thick pork chops (on or off the bone)
1 cup milk
2 cups bread crumbs
1 cup flour
¼ cup canola oil
1 large onion, sliced

(continued)

1 12-oz. jar of sliced red, green, and yellow vinegar
   peppers (I prefer Cento brand, but any brand will work.)
Salt and pepper to taste

Preheat the oven to 350°F.

Cook the potatoes in 4 to 6 cups of boiling water until tender, about ten minutes. Drain and set aside.

Rinse the pork chops and set aside. Prepare two medium bowls; fill one with the milk and the other with the flour and bread crumbs (mix well). Generously coat the pork chop in the milk and then place in the flour and bread crumb mixture. Set aside on a plate. Repeat with each chop until all pork chops are done.

Meanwhile, in a large skillet, heat the oil over medium heat. Add the sliced onions and cook for about three minutes. To the skillet, add the pork chops and cook for two minutes per side, or until both sides are golden brown. (You're not cooking them through but just enough to brown them.) Remove the chops from the skillet to a plate. Do not toss away the juices from the pan, you will need them later.

In a large roasting pan, add the pork chops, potatoes, jar of peppers (liquid and all), and 4 to 5 tablespoons of the cooking juices from the skillet. Season with the salt and pepper to taste and mix well.

Cover your pan with aluminum foil and bake for ½ hour. Remove the foil from the pan and mix with a wooden spoon.

Raise the oven temperature to 375°F and cook for approximately 15 minutes longer.

SERVES 6.

Meatballs

Al says he married me for my meatballs.
These are so good, and they're really easy to make.

9 slices white bread, divided
1½ pounds meat loaf mixture (a combination of ground
 beef, pork, and veal; ask your butcher)
1 egg
A large handful Locatelli Pecorino-Romano grated cheese
6–8 large cloves of garlic, ground fine in a food processor
1 cup milk
Salt and pepper, to taste
Vegetable oil, for shallow frying

Pulse 6 slices of the white bread in a food
processor to make homemade bread crumbs. In a
large mixing bowl, combine the homemade bread
crumbs with the meat, egg, cheese, garlic, milk,
and salt and pepper, to taste in a large bowl.

Cut the crusts off remaining 3 slices of bread.
Break the pieces up with your hands and combine
with the meat mixture. The mixture should be very
loose.

Using two soup spoons, form the meat into balls
and fry the balls in the oil until they are brown,
about five minutes.

SERVES 6.

Italian Garden Tomato Salad

Put those Jersey tomatoes to use!
Here's a simple quick recipe for an old-time family favorite.

5–6 large Jersey tomatoes (or fresh local farm stand
    tomatoes, the tastiest you can find!), cut into wedges
1 cucumber, sliced with skin on
1 green pepper, sliced
1 small red onion, thinly sliced
1 long hot pepper (optional), thinly sliced
Fresh basil, to taste
¼ cup extra virgin olive oil
Kosher salt and fresh ground pepper, to taste

Combine the tomatoes, cucumber, pepper, onion, and hot pepper in a salad bowl. Season with the fresh basil, extra virgin olive oil, kosher salt and fresh ground pepper to taste.

Nondiet watchers out there: make sure you have a nice loaf of Italian bread paired with this salad. Delicious!

Pasta e Fagioli

Albie can't get enough of this dish.
If he had his way, I'd make it every time he visited.

3–4 Tbsp. extra virgin olive oil
2 small celery ribs, chopped

(continued)

4–5 garlic cloves, chunked

A handful of diced pancetta, optional

5–6 fresh plum tomatoes, diced (or 1 16-oz. can diced
tomatoes)

1 can chicken broth

1 16-oz. can cannellini beans with liquid

2-inch rind from block of Pecorino-Romano or provolone
cheese

1 box ditalini or small shells pasta, cooked and drained

Salt and pepper, to taste

Parmigiano-Reggiano cheese, to taste

Heat the olive oil in a pan over low to medium heat. Add the celery, garlic, and the optional pancetta. Sauté until the garlic browns a bit and the celery becomes transparent.

Add the diced tomatoes, stir and let simmer for about 15 minutes.

Add the chicken broth, cannellini beans with their water, and cheese rind, and let simmer on medium heat for about 25 minutes. (When cheese rind gets mushy, remove from the pot and set aside.)

Add the pasta, top with a drizzle of the olive oil, salt and pepper to taste and grated Parmigiano-Reggiano cheese—DONE!

SERVES 4.

Struffoli

*This is an old family recipe that my grandmother
used to make. We make it only on Christmas,
and we usually fight over every last piece.*

3 eggs
½ stick melted butter
Juice from ½ fresh orange
1 cup sugar
1 tsp. vanilla
3 cups flour
½ tsp. baking powder
2 cups Crisco
2 cups honey, or to taste
Candied sprinkles, to taste

In a medium mixing bowl, whisk together the
eggs, butter, juice, sugar, and vanilla until well
blended. Add the flour and baking powder to form
a soft dough. Roll the dough into half-inch-wide
ropes. Cut the ropes into 2-inch pieces. Melt the
Crisco in the frying pan over medium to high heat.
Cook dough pieces until golden brown and set
aside. Pour as much honey as desired over the
fried dough. Shake the sprinkles over the top and
serve warm. Enjoy!

Roasted Brussels Sprouts

This is Lauren's ultimate side dish.
It's great to serve alongside chicken cutlets, or any grilled meat.

1 pound brussels sprouts, cut in half
3–4 Tbsp. olive oil
Kosher salt to taste
Fresh ground black pepper, to taste

Preheat the oven to 350°F.

In a mixing bowl, toss the brussels sprouts with the oil, and salt and pepper, to taste. Pour the mixture onto a cookie sheet and bake in the oven for 25–30 minutes.

Remember: it's Christmas presence, not Christmas presents.

As much as I spoil my kids, they're not spoiled rotten. And I bet you, if they got nothing at Christmas, they'd be fine with it as long as I kept up the traditions that we have around the holiday. They love our Christmas routine much more than any gifts they've ever received.

When they were very young, we started a tradition where the kids would get to choose the wrapping paper that Santa would wrap their gifts in. We'd all go to Friendly's and eat dinner and then get the ice cream dessert with the face on it, you know the one I mean.

After that we'd go to a store and they'd pick out their Christmas wrapping paper.

My sons are grown men now, but a week before Christmas, they'll both ask me when we're going to go buy the wrapping paper. They do it like they're indulging me, like they've outgrown the tradition. But I know deep down, if they didn't have the wrapping paper under the tree, it wouldn't be Christmas to them. Even though we're all busy, we all make time for the little things, and I love it that each of my kids will drag me to a CVS the week before Christmas so they can pick out their paper.

I spend all night on Christmas eve wrapping the presents, and the kids know which present is theirs by the wrapping paper. The funny thing is, this tradition started as a way for me to not have to do gift tags because I didn't want them to recognize my handwriting on the cards. Now it's an essential part of our holiday. This is a tradition that I love, but let me tell you, it's become a hell of a lot of work.

I don't finish cleaning up on Christmas eve until around 2:00 AM. I'm one of those crazy neat freaks, I have to wash all the dishes, put them away, and return the furniture to its original home before I go to bed. And then I have the extra task of wrapping all those friggin' presents.

I wrap around seventy-five gifts, including gifts for Al, and of course the dogs get gifts too. These days, Lauren wraps the gifts that Al buys for me, and she is in charge of putting them under the tree. I don't care if it kills me. I'm usually crying by the end of all that wrapping, I have paper cuts and my legs have gone to sleep and I never want to see a roll of sticky tape ever again. But it's completely worth it because it's a tradition they love and value even more than the gifts in those boxes.

We've always made sure the kids got just what they wanted for Christmas. You know, those must-have toys that sell out immediately and you have to pay hundreds of dollars for on eBay? Whether it was Furbys or Cabbage Patch Kids or the latest video game system, Al would make sure the kids got it. All the local businesses have their Christmas parties at The Brownstone, including the toy companies. As they booked their Christmas party, he'd say, whatever the hottest thing on the market is, bring it with you. He moved heaven and earth to get the kids what they wanted, but he always knew enough people to make it happen. There were so many things that the kids never asked for because they thought they couldn't get it, and Al would still get it for them.

But I have also learned that the simplest gifts, the ones that cost the least, become the most cherished. When my dad hit hard times while I was growing up, my mother would make us our Christmas gifts. The things my mother made me are still my most treasured possessions. She is so artistic. She makes picture frames and painted boxes. My dad made all the boys beautiful handmade wooden chests, and my mother painted them.

These days, my own kids will ask my parents to make them something for Christmas. Lauren treasures the beautiful boxes that my mom made her. There's nothing I need, there's nothing you can buy me, but for my kids to have gifts made by my parents means the world to me.

It's not about the presents, it's about the traditions, it's about family. Christmas Day has always been the one day that Al has taken off work. It's the only day of the year that I can be certain he'll be at home. And he loves it as much as I do.

On Christmas morning, he gets his robe and his camera and he takes his sweet time coming downstairs, mainly to drive the kids crazy. The more they complain, the slower he goes. It's sweet, and it's hilarious.

Then they open their gifts one at a time, in turn. It's not like a frenzy. It's very personal, and everybody sees the gifts that each other gets. I have so many photos of them opening gifts, and nothing makes me happier than seeing the look on their faces when they get a gift that touches them.

I don't think Christmas is any more important than any other holiday. It's just the holiday that has become the most important to my family. Depending on your faith and your family, you can make any day of the year the most important. That's up to you.

A while back I received a letter from a viewer whose husband was serving overseas. She wrote me that the most difficult part of this for her was that he wasn't home for Christmas and he wasn't going to be home until July. I said, that's fine—have Christmas in July. Make your own Christmas. Christmas doesn't have to be on Christmas Day. I told her to get a tree, even a fake one, and decorate it. You're making memories here, you don't need to do it by anyone else's calendar. Christmas is not December 25, it's whatever day you need it to be. It's the day when you can all be together and can create a wonderful day for your family.

I've received some sweet things from fans—and some crazy things too!

I've generally been very lucky with gifts from fans. I've heard some horror stories about weird fan mail and very strange presents, but for the most part, I just get candles, books, and jewelry. The nicest thing I ever got was a collage made for me by a viewer. She collected all these things that she knew I liked just from watching the show, and she made me a lovely collage, framed it, and sent it to me.

The strangest fan encounter happened at a BLK Water signing. I was talking to a woman who was wearing a gorgeous $900 Tory Burch jacket. I complimented her on it, and she went and bought me one and sent it to me. I couldn't believe it! It was so kind and generous. I love that coat!

Christmas is my favorite holiday. It's magical. Not because of the presents. Because of the way New York City is decorated in lights. Because the family gets together. Because the gifts appear perfectly wrapped underneath the tree. It's an important time for me, and I make sure each and every year I am completely present in the moment to take it all in.

Ask Caroline

Hey Caroline. If you know that one of your family members is in financial distress, do you think it's better to wait until they ask for help, or go to them privately and offer to help in any way you can, before they ask?

First, I would try to find out the hows and whys of the situation. I'd approach the relative and have an open and honest conversation. If you feel comfortable with lending or giving them money, then by all means help. They may be relieved and more than happy to accept your help.

I do have to warn you that if you lend the money out, you have to do it with the mind-set that you may never get the money back. I've seen this happen time and time again and it's ruined more relationships than I can count.

You have a good heart. Your family is lucky to have you. Good luck with this one.

My house is a home, not a museum. Kick your feet up and relax. If something spills, that's what mops are for.

In many ways, our house is an extension of The Brownstone. It's a place where you can come and get fed, you can laugh, you can hang out, and if you spill something, someone will clean it up for you. We always wanted our home to be informal, and welcoming. It's a nice house, but more important, it's a place where I want people to be comfortable and to have fun.

We've always welcomed all of our extended family and all of our kids' friends, at any time of the day or night. Of course, my kids took it way too far sometimes—it wasn't uncommon for me to come home and find a complete hockey game going on in my living room, or a football game being played in the upstairs hallway. It was hectic and I loved it.

I'd be making sauce in the kitchen and a football would sail by and smash a jar. A lot of things got broken. I hardly ever knew who broke what, they were all so good at covering for each other, and nobody ever admitted to breaking anything. I'd get angry when something got broken, but I'd get over it. I have a lot of sentimental things in my house, but if my house was burning down, I'd get my kids out first and then I'd rescue the photographs. The rest is just stuff.

BEHIND THE SCENES

When the camera crew arrives at my house at the beginning of each season, they turn it upside down. They take down all the pictures in my house, they hide lights in cabinets that usually house cookbooks, and they tape waxed paper over every light fixture to reduce the camera glare. They wreck my house—they've broken things, they've torn wallpaper, and they've chipped and scratched my floors and walls. When they break something, they send an appraiser to assess the damage, and then they have someone come fix it. They've damaged a lot of stuff shooting this season—the repair bill is going to be a whopper! It's all part of the job, but it's startling to see how much they have to change my home before it's ready for shooting.

For as long as we've lived in this house, it has always been filled with laughter and conversation. That's much more important to me than keeping the floors clean and the shelves spotless. If your house is a museum, dirty it up a little. Invite people over and cook up something simple and delicious. Open a few bottles of wine and have your friends drink with you in the kitchen while you cook. Informal, spontaneous nights at a friend's home can be much more special than a formal dinner party—and if you're the host, you can actually enjoy yourself a hell of a lot more.

Don't keep a guest list either—if someone is coming over and they call and ask if they can bring a friend (or two, or three), just say sure, and welcome those strangers and have the best time you can with them. Whether you like them or not doesn't matter—set them on the couch with a nice glass of wine and get to know them.

When the boys were teenagers, we would have twenty kids at a time at the house. They would have sleepovers all the time. Every year, on New Year's Eve I wouldn't know how many kids were staying over, but I always knew it was going to be a lot. They'd arrive early and we'd drive them all over to The Brownstone. I'd take all their car keys away so they couldn't drive, and at the end of the night we'd bring them all back to the house. On New Year's Day I'd

Ask Caroline

Hi Caroline! My mother-in-law has a key to our house and thinks it's OK to pop in whenever she wants. She unlocks the door and lets herself in without knocking. She says she doesn't want to startle us or wake us up, but it's uncomfortable not knowing when she's going to turn up. What's a good way to discuss this with her so that she knows she's still always welcome, but we'd like her to call and let us know she's coming first?

If you have a good relationship with her, tell her the truth. Put your arm around her and tell it like it is. Explain that you enjoy her visits but you're looking to avoid an embarrassing situation. Use a little lighthearted humor. Hug it out, but make sure she gets where you're coming from.

The bottom line is that it's your house and you're entitled to your privacy. In situations like this it's always better to act quickly so it doesn't blow up into a bigger problem with more resentment and hard feelings. Take care of this now to avoid a bigger problem down the road.

always put out a huge breakfast with coffee and bagels and there'd be twenty kids laughing and joking.

It was wonderful. I'd sit in the kitchen and read a book so they always had to get past me and I could keep an eye on them. We're talking about teenage boys and girls here. They could get loud and they were always up to something. But as much of a hassle as it could

Ask Caroline

Caroline: I'm so sick of housework and cooking. How do I get my family to do their share?

Welcome to the club! It isn't realistic to flip a switch and expect things to change overnight. I would suggest getting family members more involved in the cooking process on the weekend and make a day of it. Over the years, the responsibility of cooking has shifted from my grandparents to my parents to myself and now to my children. It was a gradual process born from spending time in the kitchen together while meals were being prepared. During conversation it became a natural progression to just start helping out. We still get together every Sunday and everyone pitches in. We have fun, we laugh, and we enjoy each other's company creating memories at the same time.

As far as keeping the house clean, well, I would say that the common areas should be respected and that's that. Set rules and boundaries and stick with them. There has to be consequences if your rules are disrespected, especially if the kids are old enough to know the difference.

Trust me, I've been known to donate my kids' favorite shoes to the homeless shelter if they've been lying around the kitchen floor after I've repeatedly asked the kids to put them away. Consequences.

As a final thought, keep in mind this is a role that you have played in your home for many years: you can't abandon it, so just revamp it a bit!

be, there's absolutely nothing in this world that makes me happier than a full house filled with the sound of laughter. I'll take that any day over sitting alone in a silent, perfectly tidy house.

My top cleaning tips

1. OxiClean is perfect for wine spills. I keep this in my back pocket pretty much.
2. Lysol wipes save my life. Whether it's a spill on a countertop, or muddy footprints, I go through a container approximately every two days.
3. The vacuum is my best friend. I have a full-size one for most of the house, but I am lost without my handheld. I'm a compulsive vacuumer!
4. Removable slipcovers and pillowcases are the absolute best. Just zip them off and wash them. And if a couch gets ruined, just buy a slipcover for it.
5. I like the brand Method, their stuff smells great, and they have cleansers for anything you can imagine!
6. When something spills take care of it right away. Never let a stain sit. Never let food stay in the pan after you're done cooking. It's just so much easier to take a minute to clean up rather than spend an hour scrubbing later in the evening.
7. I buy cheap furniture so I can replace it. Anyone with three kids knows there's no point in buying nice, expensive furniture. They'll break it just the same.

Always serve tea in a cup with a saucer.

They say God is in the details, and I say, ain't that the truth. If you take just a little bit of time to make something special, it can mean the world to someone. This attention to detail was instilled in me by my mother, and even now, at fifty-one, my mother will still haul me over the coals if I forget the littlest thing.

My mother will come to my house, and she'll ask for a cup of tea. If I serve it to her in a cup without a saucer, she'll ask for the saucer. When I bring her the saucer, she'll say, "Caroline, what did I teach you?"

My mom has always believed that it's the little things you do for your loved ones that mean the most. It's Old World wisdom at its best, and I think it's even more important than ever in this fast-paced world to remember the details, to take the time to make things special, and create traditions. I've tried my best to follow her example, but she has set the bar so high that I'm a pale imitation.

I've never seen anyone decorate for the holidays like my mother. And by holidays, I mean any and all holidays. She'll decorate for fall, Presidents' Day, Veterans Day, MLK Day, any day, season or reason. She loves it. It always makes a visit to her home special.

My mother believes that you have to prepare your house so it could become a place to create memories. I love things that make my house a home. I have decorated my house with heirlooms, things my kids made me at school, cheesy souvenirs from family vacations, and there are photos everywhere. My nephew Joseph and my niece Candice both got dressed here on their wedding day because this place feels like home to them too. I've hosted so many engagement parties and special moments in the lives of my extended family because people feel at home here. There's no bigger tribute to my home, and my mother's love of details, than that.

Sentimental treasures in my home

I have a gorgeous Lladro figure in my foyer of *The Kiss.* It's huge, and I had been lusting after it for years. The year Al decided to get it for me as a surprise, he also got incredibly ill and was admitted to the hospital just before Christmas. He was so sick, but all he cared about was getting that figure for me. He had his mother go pick it up. He made sure he got out of the hospital on December 23rd so he could give it to me. It means the world to me; it's my most precious possession.

My pinecones from the Vatican. I collected a bunch of these heavy pinecones from the garden of the Vatican. They were beside the bench where Pope John XXIII used to go and pray every day. I saw those pinecones and I scooped them up. I keep them at the center of my home in the Great Room so their energy comes up and goes all through my house.

The Christmas balls that my mom painted for me. I used to get a new one every year for my tree. I treasure them.

Framed artwork by the kids when they were little. Christopher used to think he was Picasso and he'd do these crazy paintings and give them names and everything. These paintings make me smile every time I see them.

BEHIND THE SCENES

People wrote and told me that they loved what I said at my brother's wedding. I didn't want to prepare a speech, I just wanted to speak from my heart, and I'm so honored that people liked it. What I'm glad you didn't see is that as I walked back to my seat after the speech, I totally bit it on the wet grass! It had poured the night before the wedding, and the ground was soaked and muddy. The whole time I walked up to deliver my speech, I was sure I'd fall. I was glad that it happened on my way back to my seat, and I was even happier that Bravo decided not to air my big fall.

My mother taught her daughters how to be the lady of the house, the head of the house. It wasn't a role she took lightly. We should start the day off well, she would instruct us. Shower, get dressed, fix up your appearance so you are ready to face the world. Make yourself presentable. Never say good-bye to your husband in the morning with bad breath, while you're wearing sweats and scratching at your crotch, she would say. Send your husband off with a kiss.

I know that some of you are reading it and thinking that it sounds a bit *Stepford Wives,* or even antifeminist, but it's not. It helps me to get myself all sorted out and feeling good before I start my day. If I let myself slouch around in pajamas with dirty hair and bad breath until lunchtime, it would depress me. I'd start to go downhill. By tending to the details of appearance first thing in the morning, I feel good about myself and I feel excited to get things done, every day. My mother believes that God is in the details, and that as long as we always take a second to make something as special as it can be, people will appreciate and enjoy our efforts.

In my world, it's the simplest things, like a smile and an I-love-you cost nothing. All of my kids have been raised knowing this, and they have all embraced my mother's traditions. My boys are

Ask Caroline

Hi Caroline, I'm a mother of two extremely active, adorable kids (ages two and four). How can I give them my constant attention while juggling everything else I have to do—housework, cooking, cleaning, and my full-time job?

The old saying is true: a mother's work is never done. You can't be all things to all people at all times. Take a step back and give yourself breathing room. Children don't need "constant" attention—that will only lead to separation anxiety whenever you leave the room. Supervise them, but teach them to play on their own.

Plan your weekly routine, and stick to it. Prepare for school days on the night before, do your housework a little at a time rather than in one tedious lump. Stick to your schedule, and make sure you leave plenty of time for you and your husband. Me time is good for the soul—and it helps save your sanity on those tough days.

You're not alone. There are millions out there just like you. Your kids will grow and become more responsible sooner than you think, so stop now and smell the roses. And the poop . . . and the spit-up. You'll miss it when it's gone!

sentimental. They'll save a note I leave them, they'll save a fortune cookie from a special dinner. I'm very sentimental too. A picture of a moment captured can melt my heart. I have every piece of stupid macaroni jewelry they ever made for me. I have every note they ever wrote me, and pictures that they drew for me. When we lived in

Wayne, there was a gift shop on the corner, and every week they'd all go there and buy me a gift and I still have every single one of them. They'd get me little statues of boys praying or a little rabbit or some dried flowers. The little things mean the most to me; I will cherish them always.

PART III

KIDS

For spoiled kids, my kids worked their asses off.

I'll say it before you think it. I spoil my kids. I do. And I'm not ashamed of it. Nothing makes me happier than to treat them with something special. I've bought my kids cars, and they've always had the latest technological gadgets. If you watch the show, you may even think I give them too much. But before you judge, here's something you might not know. While I'm the first to admit that I can overindulge them at times, as a parent, it was one of my top priorities to make sure my kids also developed a strong work ethic. Even from a young age, my kids have understood the value of hard work.

Because Al worked such long hours, the kids were frequently at The Brownstone to visit him. It's our family's second home. It was clear to them that while Daddy wished he could be playing, he had to work to support the family.

The boys started pitching in alongside their dad at The Brownstone when they were in elementary school. It really was something else to watch them. Eight-year-old Christopher was so proud of his job, polishing all the bottles at the bar for ten cents a bottle; he even made himself a business card. All the labels had to be facing forward, he kept a tab on how many bottles he polished, and if he got his count wrong, he didn't get paid. If the bottles weren't facing straight, no cash. It was so adorable to watch him, keeping checks and balances, acting like a little man.

Albie was on cleanup patrol. If someone threw up he had to go mop it up. Some people said we were being harsh by giving him this job, but I didn't see it that way. My kids are spoiled rotten, but when it comes to working hard, they don't get any special treatment. It was important to us as parents that the boys didn't automatically get cushy jobs just because they were the kids of the owners. We made sure that both boys had to work their way up. They started polishing bottles, then moved up to cleaning ashtrays and sweeping up cigarette butts outside. Not that they complained about it. I didn't have to twist the boys' arms to work. They wanted to, and they took pride in their jobs. I was such a proud mommy.

When they proved themselves, the boys were graduated to loading trucks, working as valets, and finally managing the valet, handling hirings and firings. Once, when Christopher was managing the valet, one of the drivers hit a car in the parking lot. For insurance reasons, Christopher had to be deposed, at eighteen.

When the insurance adjuster asked Chris to give his deposition, Chris asked if Albert would come into the questioning room with him. "Why, do I manage the valet?" Albert asked. You should have seen poor Chris's eyes widen. But Al felt that Christopher needed to understand how serious a responsibility it was to be giving a deposition. Chris summoned the courage and did it by himself. He told the truth, he knew the facts and he stepped up and handled it like a man.

I was incredibly proud of Christopher, because he literally worked his way to the very top. By the end of his time at The Brownstone, Chris had a desk beside his father. He wore a suit and oversaw the entire operation, just like his dad.

Lauren worked around The Brownstone too. She didn't do the hard manual labor that the boys did. But she checked coats, she took reservations, and then she started helping with the wedding parties. I remember once she came home and told me she'd had to put her head under a bride's dress to fix her stockings. *"That's your job, Lauren,"* I said to her. She just had to suck it up. But she did love the job, every minute of it. Well, maybe not that minute . . .

Lauren was also always expected to help me around the house. She did laundry, she cleaned the refrigerator. She made the boys' beds. The boys never made their beds, and she would complain about it, but I always told her that a girl needs to learn to be a good wife and mother. Call me old-fashioned, I don't mind. But I was raised to believe it's more important for the girl to learn to keep a house than her brothers. I was very tough on Lauren in the house, and Al was harder on the boys at work.

The kids were paid for the work they did at The Brownstone, but we never paid them an allowance for the work they did around the home. It's not something I believe in—paying your children just because? For things they should be doing as members of the family anyway? It just didn't make sense to me, and I didn't want to send the message that they could expect money once a week just because they did something that they should be doing anyway. Sometimes the kids had nothing in their pockets, sometimes they had a hundred dollars. But they never got paid for nothing. It's my firm belief that when kids have expendable cash that's when problems start—who knows what they'll do with that extra money, especially when they reach a certain age and pot, alcohol, and other drugs enter the picture.

If the kids asked for money, we'd ask what for? If they wanted clothes, I'd go with them to buy the clothes. If they were going out, they had to tell us where they were going and they had to call us and let us know where they were. We never just gave them going-out money with no questions asked. But they were also never without. We got them the clothes they wanted, and they always had enough money to hang out with their friends.

All of my kids have inherited our work ethic, and not one of them is a spoiled brat. When Christopher started the eighth grade, he saw a Rolex watch on a billboard, and he had to have it. He told his father that was the one thing he wanted. It cost four thousand dollars at the time. It was very expensive, and my husband told Christopher that it was fine if he wanted it, but he had to work for it. We wouldn't buy it for him.

Christopher was thirteen or fourteen, and he became obsessed with working for that watch. He never stopped, he was relentless. And by the time he graduated eighth grade, that summer, he had saved enough to buy it. It was just incredible to see as a parent. I went with him to the jewelers as he made the final payment, and took that watch and put it on his wrist. I'll never forget the expression on his face. It was the first time I looked at him and saw the man that he would become. I was so proud I cried.

I was reminded of Christopher's watch recently when the boys moved to Hoboken. When Christopher was faced with having to pay $300 a month for a garage, he decided to sell his car and just take public transportation. When he comes to visit me, he either rides with somebody or he takes the train to Ridgewood, and somebody picks him up. He's become a smart businessman.

If kids want things that are out of reach, don't kill that dream. If you can't afford to get it for them, show them that if they work, they can get it. All dreams are attainable if you want to work for it.

Because they always were putting in the work at The Brownstone and at home, it was easy to spoil them. They were good kids. And because of our parenting choices to push them to work hard and to not give them an allowance, I believe they understood the value of hard work and money better than a lot of their friends.

One thing that makes me proud and lets me know we did the right thing is the fact that all three of my kids have a very strong work ethic. They have all grown into hardworking adults, and I still love to treat them to indulgences every now and then. But if you see one of them walk by some trash on the ground at The Brownstone and not pick it up, you let me know.

Talking about sex with your kids may be uncomfortable, but it's easier than an unplanned pregnancy.

I've never understood why people think it's hard to talk about sex with their kids. We potty train our kids, don't we? The sex talk can be as funny, messy, and silly as toilet training. But it's just as essential.

The way we did it in our house was we first let the teachers at school take care of teaching the kids the nuts and bolts of sex. They get to hear all the funny stuff in a roomful of their friends, and it's much less mortifying than hearing it from me or their dad.

After that, Albert and I would follow up to let the kids know about the responsibility and the respect that go along with being sexually active. Al and I were always blunt and open with our kids. Once, I found a condom in Albie's room, which told me he was either having sex or thinking about having sex. So I confronted him about it. I explained to him that I knew he was of the age to start hanging out with girls, but I wanted him to always respect a girl and never force himself on a girl. I wanted him to always treat women the way he liked to be treated, with kindness and empathy. That was the mom's version of "the talk" with my son.

Then I called Al and told him I'd found the condom and that it was time for him to have his version of that talk with Albie. I don't know what Al said to him, it wasn't ever my business. The open dialogue that we kept at home revolved around our kids respecting themselves and the people they were getting intimate with. It was never as open in my parents' home, but that was a different time, and it was important for me to be more forthcoming with my own kids.

As a mother, my message to Lauren was even more important. I was very matter-of-fact with her, telling her that she wasn't a pincushion. I told her she never wanted to be the girl that guys don't respect, the girl that guys talk about but never give the time of day. Anyone with a daughter needs to teach her that self-respect is the most important thing to have before you start to even think about sex. And teaching self-respect is something that happens in more than just one talk. You have to be vigilant with daughters. We all know how persuasive boys can be. It's incredibly important to let a daughter know that her self-worth does not revolve around her popularity with boys.

It's ridiculous to pretend that your kids aren't going to experiment with sex. Sure, some kids may not, but most of them will, and it's up to you to make sure they know about contraception and also about HIV and other diseases. Seriously, if you do a good enough job of *that* talk, it'll scare them off sex for at least a couple years.

I was always the mother that all the kids came to with their sexual problems. Lauren would bring them to me and tell me their problems—this girl needed a morning-after pill, this girl was raped, this girl might be pregnant. I'd sit and talk to these girls and boys about their problems and then I'd take them to their parents.

What I found most frequently was that these kids were just so terrified to talk about these issues with their own parents. And it just broke my heart to see them so alone, and so scared. Just because of sex. When I took them to their parents, it was never as bad as they anticipated. Parents were all teenagers once, and they know what goes on.

At a certain age, there was a shift in how we communicated with the kids. I started pulling back with the boys. They'd go on spring break, and all I asked of them was a phone call each day to let me know they were alive. I never asked any questions about what they were up to. It's not a mother's place to be so invasive. They'd call to check in, and I'd just say I'm glad you're having a good time. Later on, Albert would come home and say he'd talked to Albie and gotten the real story about his wild night, and we'd laugh. And that's fine, my husband knew the daddy version and I got the mommy version.

When my sons turned eighteen, my husband would get them a hotel room if they needed it. Albert would tell me if one of our sons wasn't coming home on a particular night, and as long as I knew he was safe, I was OK with it. I wouldn't call him or bother him or ask him about it afterward. I recognized that my son was becoming a man, and that the respect between us was a two-way street. I learned to respect their privacy.

Even with Lauren, she's twenty-three and she's been with Vito for three years, but when he comes over he can't sleep in her room. She has to respect this house. She's in a long-lasting relationship with a guy she's going to marry, but I have my boundaries.

I admit that I'm stricter on Lauren than I am on the boys. Albie is now living with a girl, and when they come over and stay, I let her sleep in his room. But they're living together. That's different. If Lauren was living with Vito they could sleep together when they visited too, but they aren't. It doesn't work like that.

These days, instead of talking about sex, the boys ask my opinion of the girls they date. Lauren is loyal to Vito, and I don't pry into their bedroom. My kids have all made it through to adulthood with no unplanned pregnancies or other sexual problems. This makes me glad we were always open to talking to our kids about sex. Any parent who tries to raise her kids in denial of sex is just asking for them to get screwed!

Principal, I *want* you to punish my kids.

From the minute my kids went off to school, I knew the game had changed. They were no longer completely under my care and guidance. They would be influenced now not only by what I taught them at home, but also by what they learned from their teachers. The time had come for me to share part of my parenting duties with my kids' new influences, so I enlisted the help of teachers, principals, guidance counselors. That's what they're there for! As a parent, I let the teachers teach, that's their number one role. But I did value the guidance they gave me, and I always looked to them to help me become a better parent myself.

Teachers loved the way Al and I parented our kids. They thought it was refreshing and uncommon. We weren't the parents that said "oh, not my child!" We were the ones that said "if they did it, pun-

Ask Caroline

Caroline, I'm the mother of a nine-year-old boy, and I was wondering what you think is the appropriate age to discuss the topic of sex.

That's a tough one. It depends on the child. Some kids mature faster than others, both physically and emotionally. Watch your son as he develops and make your decision about when to talk sex based on his maturity level, not his age.

If he starts asking questions, always answer them honestly. When my kids were in fifth grade, they had a program designed for mother/daughter and father/son. The school nurse explained human anatomy and puberty, and even though it was awkward for the kids, at least they were there with a parent. If your school has that program, use it. If it doesn't, suggest it.

By the time your son goes to middle school he should have a basic understanding of things. Kids today are more advanced than we believe, and it's our job as parents to guide them down a responsible path.

I was lucky to have Al for a partner, as there are some things it's easier for a son to talk about with his dad. Al and I were very vocal with our kids when it came to using protection and acting responsibly. The bottom line is this: I'd rather have an uncomfortable conversation with my child about sex than have an issue with my child because I didn't.

ish them." They appreciated that we respected their position as educators.

All three of our kids were very different in school. Chris was a cutup and a smart-ass (in a good way). Lauren was quiet, but deadly. She knew which teachers to schmooze, so she never got into trouble. Albie was serious, he always wanted to please the teachers, but he was also mischievous. And the teachers were invaluable to us with all three. I e-mailed their teachers all the time, so I always knew when the kids had homework, even when they told me they didn't!

BEHIND THE SCENES

My kids love to mess with the camera guys. We've been around our crew so much, they're like family to us, which means they're all prime targets for practical jokes. The worst is Chris, he's always up to something. Once, during our time in Punta Cana, the cameraman was walking backward, filming Chris.. What he couldn't see was that he was heading toward a pool. Chris didn't say a thing, he just kept walking and doing his scene. At the very last second, a producer grabbed the cameraman and saved him from plunging into the pool with a $150,000 camera on his shoulder.

When Christopher was in middle school he was befriended by a kid with a bad reputation. The boy came by the house once or twice, and I told Christopher that I wasn't a fan and that he should reconsider the friendship. During this time, I contacted the school's guidance counselor. He had a talk with Christopher to reinforce my point of view while giving his. He kept an eye on Chris during lunch and recess. Chris fought me on my desire for him to find a new friend for a week or two but then he started to understand where I was coming from and eventually ended the friendship.

By enlisting the help of the school community and getting them more involved in my child's well-being, I created a win-win scenario: I could be a better parent, and my son stayed out of trouble and could focus on his schooling.

Lauren was very quiet—she only came out of her shell after

Ask Caroline

Caroline, I don't know what to do. My only son just told me that he has joined the army. I'm shocked and I can't stop crying. My whole life revolves around him, and it feels like a piece of my heart is torn out. I'm very grateful for the men and women who defend our country, but I don't want my son to be one of them. How can I handle this?

Be proud of your son. Joining the military takes courage and character. Don't let him leave with a heavy heart; show him you are proud of him. It's probably going to be the hardest moment of your life, but you have to put your best mom face on and send him off with love and a smile. OK—a teary smile is fine.

I commend all the servicemen and -women who protect us, but I agree that we often forget about the families and friends they leave behind. Throw yourself into something positive for him. There are numerous organizations you can join (visit www.troopsupport.com for more info), and you'll be able to feel connected to your son while he's away.

Good luck to you and God bless your son and all those who serve to protect our country.

high school—but she was also very popular. She moved among the cliques, with friends in all of them even though she didn't belong to any of them. The only issues I had with Lauren were the typical "mean girl" issues we're all too familiar with—hey, even on the *Real Housewives* this issue has a way of rearing its ugly head (if only *we* had guidance counselors!). Every now and then, I would ask the guidance counselor if she had noticed any bullying, so I could keep tabs on any situations that might crop up. Lauren was lucky, and she learned to stand up for herself early on. She understood that mean girls are only as powerful as you let them be. This motto has also been my mantra for the entire time I've been doing the show. These days, Lauren is almost as bulletproof as I am!

Now Albie was a different story. In third grade Albie came home one day and started bragging that he got away with not completing a report. Instead of using the month he was given to work on the assignment, on the day it was due he charmed the teacher and convinced her to let him get up in front of the class and sing a song and tell some jokes in place of handing in written work. I couldn't believe it, but she had said yes! I mean, he had the balls to get up and do whatever he had to do to get a grade, and he did it. But the bottom line is that he didn't do the job he was supposed to do. I told him I was proud of him that he'd thought on his feet but ultimately he hadn't done his assignment.

He was supposed to have done a report on tigers. So I told him he was going to do a report on tigers for the toughest teacher around—me! I went with him to the library and sat with him while he checked out books and made notes and photocopied pictures. I needed him to know that being a smart-ass wasn't something he could rely on for the rest of his life.

Sometimes Mom could be tougher than the teachers, and with good reason. Like the time the boys were playing wall ball at school. Wall ball is a popular game that kids in Jersey play, but it was banned at school. Albie and his friends broke the rules, played, Albie ended up getting hurt, and the boys got caught. The principal called me to tell me he was going to suspend all the kids who were playing except Albie, because he was home from school with a concussion. "No, no, no," I said. "Wait 'til Albie gets back to school and suspend them all at once!"

The principal couldn't believe what he was hearing—a parent asking for her child to be suspended? But I was adamant. Just because he got hurt didn't mean he shouldn't be punished. Poor Albie? No, Albie was just as guilty as the other boys. He went back to school, and they all got punished together.

Once kids hit middle-school age, they're old enough to take responsibility for getting their assignments turned in on time, and they're generally better able to stick up for themselves. I backed off a lot at that time, but I still got updates from my kids every single day regarding class participation, homework assignments, and anything else going on in their lives. From then on, teachers played a small part when it came to discipline and punishment, but I was never afraid to enlist their help when I needed it.

Be a parent now. You can't press "rewind" later.

Your kids aren't born with a rewind button. If only! From the moment you find out you're carrying that baby, your life changes forever (in more ways than not drinking, smoking . . .), because you are now fully responsible for another person. For me, I knew being a mom was more than making sure my children were healthy and happy. I also wanted to be there for them every step of the way. You only get one shot with each kid, and I didn't want to miss any moment.

I've worked my entire life, and I've worked hard. But I was able to find the right balance between being a mommy and being a businesswoman. Switching between the two wasn't always easy, but it was important for me to be completely present when I was with my children. When the kids started school I sold real estate. I would get up early every morning to spend quality time with them before they headed off, but as soon as I dropped them at school, I switched into professional mode. I'd race all over North Jersey showing houses and taking clients around. It was not always easy to get up so early, but I made a point to keep a clockwork schedule, arranging my days in such a way so I was always done working in time to be out front of the school waiting for them at three o'clock.

From the moment I picked them up at school, I was Mommy again. I was home with them for the rest of the day, and when I was

Ask Caroline

Dear Caroline, What are the best and worst things you've done in regards to parenting your children? And does your faith have anything to do with that?

Wow, what a great question. I wish I had a simple answer for you. The best thing I've done is to treat my children as individuals and never compare one to the other. I can't answer the worst thing. I would only feel like something was the worst if we'd failed our kids in some way. We've made mistakes along the way, but I can't think of anything that qualifies as a specific worst thing. Al and I put our hearts and souls into raising our kids, so I have no regrets. Faith plays a part in every aspect of our lives, but we don't throw our hands up and leave things up to just faith. We always work at things.

home with them, I was really *with* them. That means I put my phone down and turned off the computer. We would play, we'd talk about what they'd done that day; we'd eat and laugh.

When I tucked the kids into bed each night, I would once again switch back into being a businesswoman. I'd get on the computer, send e-mails to clients, set up appointments for showings, and co-ordinate complicated real estate sales until Al got home from The Brownstone. Then he and I would have our time together. I barely slept and I was always tired, but I was happy and I felt like I was there for my kids.

Every now and then, we'd get a sitter and have a night to our-selves. We'd let the kids stay up a bit later on those nights, and make it a little special for them. We generally only did this occasionally to catch up with other adult friends or see a movie that wasn't right for the kids. Most of the time, though, I wanted my kids around me.

In the back of my mind, I always knew my kids were truly only "mine" for a fixed time before they became adults and started lives of their own. Being aware of that influenced the decisions I made as a parent. I never wanted to miss those special moments with them, and some of the most memorable times were the ordinary nights spent around our kitchen table.

I also never wanted to vacation without them. Many of the other local kids went on these all-summer-long trips by themselves to different countries while their parents would have a kid-free sum-mer. Everybody got a break, but I never understood it. Because Al worked so much, being able to have time together as a family was always so precious. I never even sent my kids away to camp, partially because Italians don't do camp, but also because we went on family vacations. Road trips. Up to Cape Cod, down to Cape May. They were great times. I will treasure those memories forever.

Because I understood that my kids' childhoods were fleeting, and I knew I could not press some button to turn back the clock, it never felt like a chore for me to go and watch a hockey game, a school play, or a dance recital. I didn't feel obligated to do these things; I wanted to. Every parent knows how tedious a school play can be when your own kid isn't actually on the stage. But as soon as we would get home, it was always clear that my kids were thrilled that I'd been there for them. We could then talk, laugh, and gossip about their performances. I still remember watching Lauren, wearing some crazy outfit while hip-hop dancing to 'N Sync. She had the biggest smile while she pulled off all these complicated moves.

I hardly ever missed anything that my kids did, and I still deeply regret the things I did miss. I couldn't be at one of Lauren's dance recitals when she was six because my sister had a destination wedding—no kids invited. I felt terrible about it. I went to Lauren's full dress rehearsal the night before we left and made sure every member of my husband's family was at the actual recital.

It didn't matter. Lauren was so devastated that Al and I weren't there she never wanted to dance again. She literally stopped dancing and didn't pick it up again until middle school. She still talks about it to this day. And it breaks my heart like it just happened yesterday— especially since that sister's marriage didn't last!

These days, as young adults, all three of them want to spend time

My top five moments as a parent

1. Watching Albie graduate from Fordham
2. Watching Lauren develop Cafface and open her first store and gain self-confidence
3. Watching Chris leave his father's business to start his own
4. I was there for each kid's first steps and first words. Nothing is better than those memories!
5. Watching my three children navigate the celebrity world with grace

with Al and me. We have a natural, tight bond that was built by those hours upon hours of togetherness. We experienced every laugh, tear, and triumph as a family. And now we have a friendship that honestly means everything in the world to me.

That's why I always tell my friends to drop everything for their kids when they're young. You get one shot at it. Your baby will only ever get one childhood. You can't press "rewind," and the memories are a million times better than years of regret.

The secret to being good parents is to never disagree with each other in front of your kids.

People are always asking me two things—what are my secrets to a long happy marriage, and what are my secrets to raising three good kids? The first thing that comes to my mind actually answers both: Al and I have never disagreed in front of the kids. Ever.

We understood from very early on that if kids sense a weakness between their parents, they'll exploit it. Kids are crafty, and they are always testing authority. If they think they can pit one parent against the other to get their own way, they'll do it. If you show your kids even the slightest crack between you and your husband, they will manipulate it like crazy, and before long, you'll be at war with your spouse!

Before you even think about having kids, make sure that you and your spouse are on exactly the same page when it comes to how you'll raise your kids. You need to know that you both have the same standards on exactly what's appropriate for your children and what's not.

The easiest way to start the united front of parenting is to answer every request from your child by asking what your spouse already said. Did they already ask Dad if they could do something? And if so, what did he say? And no matter what Al had said as his answer, even if I didn't agree, I would go along with it.

Of course we held different opinions at times on how to handle the kids. The worst thing we ever disagreed on was curfew. Chris started working long hours at The Brownstone in his teenage years, so if he wanted to hang out with his friends, he had to do it late at night when he was done with work.

My husband had grown up working at The Brownstone, so he understood Chris's request and OK'ed a 2:00 AM curfew as a result. I have never understood parents who think it's fine for kids under twenty-one to stay out that late. What's a nineteen-year-old kid doing out at 1:00 AM? Get into trouble, that's what.

I didn't react when Chris told me that his father had approved a 2:00 AM curfew. I waited until Al got home to discuss it privately. I explained my thoughts, but this time, Al wouldn't budge. He wanted Chris to work but also to be able to enjoy himself, the way Albert himself had done when he was a teenager. So we came up with a compromise: Chris would have to tell us where he wanted to go, and we'd approve late nights on a per-case basis. That system worked well for us and it didn't undermine my husband's original decision either.

We saw so many parents who used their children as pawns when they were fighting, trying to buy their children's affection at the expense of their relationship with the other parent. Al and I never wanted to be like that. No matter how bad things can get in a marriage, it's never appropriate to pin all the hard calls on your husband just so you can play good cop. Even if you come to hate your spouse, you have to respect that your partner is just as much your kid's parent as you are.

We were so careful to never disagree that we had a rule: if the kids sprung something on us that we weren't prepared for, we'd tell them we'd let them know later. We'd meet up in private and discuss it, and we'd deliver our verdict later. To this day, when the kids ask Al about something, his answer will always be, "What did your mother say?"—and I'm beyond proud to say that my husband of thirty years and I have never fought about something to do with our kids.

Overprotective parents raise underprepared kids.

Kids are kids, not idiots. I keep seeing "experts" on TV talking about how it's important to shield kids from the harsh realities of the world when they're too young to understand. This kind of advice makes me see red. Children have to realize that there is hurt in the real world, and it's up to the parents to make sure they're prepared to deal with it.

You need to raise warriors. Kids can't win every contest or be student of the month every month. They have to be benched on the team and earn their spot to play. They aren't going to be invited to every birthday party, and that's OK. Not everyone in the world is going to like them, that's the truth. It's your job as a parent, especially when your children are very young, to get them ready for the day when you're not there to defend them. If you keep your children in a protective bubble, they will never survive in the real world.

I'll never forget when the kids were younger and one of their friend's parents was shocked by my decision to allow them to watch *Rugrats*! This parent told me that she had banned her kids from watching the show because the cartoon characters bickered and called each other "stupid"—I was incredulous. I looked this woman straight in the eye. "What the hell are you talking about, lady?" I said. Life is not all lollipops and roses. To not prepare your child for the real world is the biggest disservice you could ever do to your children.

Our kids watched *Bambi* and every single Disney movie ever

made—and when there was a sad part we talked about it. It's crazy to me when parents won't let their kids watch this classic movie. I truly believe they're robbing them of an experience that is an integral part of modern childhood. It's not a violent bloody portrayal— it's a sad fact of life, beautifully handled. My kids understood that sometimes sad things happen in life, but life goes on and what matters most is how you handle those unfortunate situations.

From a young age our kids were exposed to many of the harsher realities in life, including the concept of being homeless. On the morning of December 26 each year, we asked the kids to go through their room and pull out anything they didn't want anymore, from clothes to toys to books. They gave me their goods and we'd put their castoffs on a table at The Brownstone during the charity lunch later that day. The homeless kids would throw themselves at the table. They'd be so excited to get something that my kids had thrown away. We'd make them see that something that they had discarded was making another child so happy, that was the lesson we wanted them to learn. We pushed our kids to go and introduce themselves to these kids, to talk to them and learn about them. Through this tradition our children learned that there were those out there who were less fortunate than us, their home life wasn't as comfortable, and they struggled more than we did.

As much as we were open with the kids, there were things that we never talked about with them. It's never appropriate to talk about your private life with your kids. And they should never be exposed to things that are too emotionally complex for them, like sexual issues or trouble between their parents. They don't need to know that their aunt is having an affair or that their uncle can't make his rent this month.

We never let them sit at a table of adults and join adult conversation. We tried to always be real with them, but we also wanted their childhoods to last as long as possible.

I've received a lot of criticism for my take on parenting over the years. Some might say I'm too tough, or even that I'm a bitch. I just think I'm smart enough to realize that I'm not going to live forever and my kids need to be able to live without me.

Trust me, the longer you shield them, the worse it's gonna be.

I'm your mother, not your friend.

Fans of the show are always telling me how much they love the relationship I have with my kids. "I wish I was friends with my kids the way you are with yours," they say. But I always stop them right there and correct them. I'm not friends with my kids. I'm their mom. There's a difference, and understanding that boundary is essential to good parenting.

You're not pals with your kids. You don't hang out and gossip with them. You don't want to be cool like them or fit right in with their friends. You're their parent; don't try to be their friend. I love my parents. I'm over fifty years old and they're both still with me, and I'm blessed to have them around. But even as an adult, with grown children of my own, I do not consider my parents to be my friends. They're still my parents, and what I get from that relationship is better than any friendship in the world.

I've seen situations where a parent's desire to be friends with their kid ends up creating a power structure where the child has the upper hand. Once this happens, all bets are off. Never let the tail wag the dog.

Viewers of the show will recognize this from the battle that Jacqueline had with her daughter. I do agree that it's harder for parents going through a divorce to not let the child cross into friend territory. Many single parents work too hard to have a social life, and the child becomes their world. But a time comes when a parent has to be a parent, and as we've seen time and time again, this is a tough road to get back to once you've crossed into friend category. It can be heartbreaking to have to start from scratch to rebuild those boundaries.

Ask Caroline

Dear Caroline: I want to build a relationship with my daughter based on trust. Where do you draw the line between being too friendly with your children, yet encouraging them to come to you when they need to?

Trust is an integral part of any relationship, but you have to remember this is a relationship between a parent and a child: you are responsible for their safety and welfare until they are out on their own. There must be rules and boundaries that are respected by your child.

I think a lot of parents put too much emphasis on the word "friend"; how about we say "relationship" instead? It's simple: if you want a strong relationship, you have open communication, you talk to your child, listen when they speak, ask them questions, become engaged in true conversation. Tell them "I love you" every single day. Spend time with them doing simple things like cooking a meal together or going to the movies. During those moments tell them stories about your life and see if it relates to theirs in some way, for example, "when my first boyfriend broke up with me I was devastated." By doing this you are creating a bond that is built on communication.

It's during these times that you can speak to them with truth and make them understand that you were young once too; you will understand that they will want to try things, and that some decisions they make may be foolish ones. Most important, you must stress that there is nothing that they can't come and discuss with you. They have to know that your love is unconditional.

If you're looking for the key to building the perfect parent/child relationship, just observe the way your kids are with their grandparents. Nobody expects their grandparents to be their friends, there's already a built-in respect for that relationship. Gradually transfer that relationship to the way your kids deal with you. The boundaries are basically the same. When your kids are grown, they'll be grateful that you are their parent and not their friend. Friends come and go, but your parents are yours in a way that can't be replicated in your life. It's the best relationship in the world.

I raised kids, not monsters.

There's no such thing as a kid who was born bad. To make a rotten kid, it takes a rotten parent. If you see a kid melting down at the

How to argue

When you're trying to reason with your child, sometimes it's not just what you say, but how you say it.

The more you scream, the easier it is for the kid to block you out. It's white noise to them, even though it's exhausting for you. They can outlast you. The secret is to always talk to them calmly. We didn't raise our voices at our kids, and we never called them names when we were angry with them. I didn't want them thinking it was OK for them to talk to others like that.

As tough as we were as parents, we never let our kids go to bed thinking that we were angry at them. No matter what they did, we would go into their room at bedtime and tell them that we loved them and that we hoped they understood why they were in trouble.

Chris: in his own words

I was probably the worst behaved of the three kids in my family, and as a result, I got punished the most. I truly believed I was invincible when I was little, in some ways I still do. I was always up for anything, and I was never as good at covering my tracks as I thought I was.

My parents used the threat of punishment way more than they used actual punishment. The key was that all three of us knew that if we pushed it too far, the threat would become a reality. That's what made it work.

I pushed the envelope pretty hard when I was a kid, but because of my parents' discipline, I always expected my actions to have consequences. I never knew how severe they would be, but I was always aware that if I was doing something wrong, I'd pay for it later.

They'd threaten to beat the shit out of us, when we were really bad, but they never did it. The threat was that they might. That's why whenever Mom said I was going to The Brownstone, I knew I'd gone too far, and I knew I was in for it. The drive to The Brownstone was like the Green Mile for me. It was awful.

Getting punished at The Brownstone was the absolute worst thing that could happen to you. Just being yelled at by my dad is scary enough. But it was humiliating for that to happen at his place of work in front of everyone else.

That time I got stranded at the Meadowlands, it made perfect sense to me to do what I did. My gym teacher at the time hated me. He told my friend and I that we couldn't go to the ball game with everyone

(continued)

else. This only made me completely determined that we had to be at that game.

I knew we'd get in trouble for it, but I needed this teacher to know that we beat him. So we got tickets, we got a ride to the game, and I figured that the teacher would have to let us on the bus to get home. I was wrong.

I made up a whole bullshit story about it, and it didn't work. My mom knew it wasn't true, and that was it. Lying and getting caught always made the punishment worse.

The funny thing was always that my dad hated disciplining us, but he knew he had to do it. I don't even know if my mom knows, but Dad would always say, "I hate having to do this to you guys, but it has to happen." He would say that Mom was flipping out and he had to discipline us, even though he would have done the same thing at our age.

I grew up in an area with a lot of old money. A lot of my friends' parents never disciplined or screamed at their kids. A lot of my friends were huge punks, they were really out of control, and they never got in trouble for it. I look back now at people like that, and I look at all the opportunities that they've wasted. They were all handed jobs as assistants that paid $80,000 a year right out of high school while I was paid ten cents a bottle to polish bottles at The Brownstone.

Those kids dropped out of college after four months and didn't get in any trouble for it. Those kids with no fear of discipline really never found their way, and they

(continued)

never ended up respecting anyone. I can name fifteen kids who came from that background who have been to rehab or jail. That's what makes my life different. We're not the best kids in the world, but we've never done drugs or gotten into serious trouble.

I always remember than whenever my dad did have to punish us, he'd always hug us afterward and say, "I love you, I'm sorry I had to do that but one day you'll understand."

As I get older, I'm starting to understand. And, when I'm a parent, and I care for my kids as much as my parents cared for me, I'll understand completely.

mall, look at how the parent is reacting. Kids copy their parents. If that kid is a brat, you can bet the parent is just as much of a brat, if not worse.

From the time your child hits the terrible twos, you have to be the boss. Kids will start testing you, and it's up to you to stand firm and let them know what behavior is acceptable and what isn't. It's also up to you to set a good example. I always wanted my kids to be welcomed at my friends' houses, to make a good impression. They knew that when we went visiting, they needed to be polite, they needed to be well behaved, and they needed to be quiet. I was raised that way and I was damn sure my kids were going to be raised the same way.

The place I see some of the worst behavior from children is at The Brownstone. Parents start drinking and acting reckless, and guess what, the kids follow suit. The parents stop watching their kids, and the kids go crazy, spilling food, breaking things, racing into other rooms and upsetting other patrons. I am shocked by how careless some parents are. If your kids don't know how to behave at a public event, you shouldn't be bringing them to one. I was always horrified by the thought of someone looking at my kids and saying, "Look at those little beasts!"

BEHIND THE SCENES

People always ask if our visits to restaurants on the show are spontaneous or set up in advance, and the answer is, yes, they're prearranged. To shoot at almost any location, you need signed contracts and insurance—we even have agreements so we can shoot in our own homes! The producers have to work with the restaurants to make sure that we are legally able to shoot there. However, even though the owners know we're coming, the patrons usually don't, so sometimes you can see people staring or freaking out or texting their friends in the background. It's hilarious.

With grandmotherhood (hopefully) just around the corner, I know my grandkids are going to be angels too, because they're going to have my kids for parents, and Grandma and Grandpa are going to be watching from the wings.

I'd rather you said *fuck* than did heroin.

There's a correct way to speak your mind. Be yourself in your own home. But be polite and respectful. And I've taught my kids the difference. As a parent, you have to pick your battles, and swearing is really not a big deal. As long as it never happens in front of Grandma!

To ground or not to ground

In my opinion grounding is lazy parenting. It doesn't do anything in terms of teaching a kid a lesson. Any kid can fake good behavior for a week. I used to confiscate things from the kids. If they were naughty, I'd take their Nintendo, their cell phone, whatever they were into at the time. I never hid the thing I confiscated. I'd set it right in the middle of the kitchen table! We'd eat dinner with a damn Nintendo on the table, just to needle them. During dinner, I'd ask Albie why his Nintendo was on the table. I'd bring it up all the time. It was hard to keep a straight face, but it's a really effective punishment!

I never gave the thing back until I was certain that the kid had learned from his or her mistake. Sometimes I'd keep the thing on the table for a week, sometimes it would sit there for a month. Sometimes, Al would get the Nintendo and play with it in front of the kids, and then put it back on the table. We messed with them, but they learned what it cost them to screw up. It's not easy, but it's effective, and after a while, you'll notice that your kids are behaving a lot better.

I see it like this. Sure my kids my say *fuck* every now and then, but they're good kids, who work hard and stay away from trouble. Wouldn't you rather that, than a kid who has the cleanest mouth in the world but is hiding a drug problem from you?

Kids need to know that it's wrong to say "where's my fuckin' dinner?" or "get the fuck outta here" but it's fine to say, "Oh, Ma, the craziest fuckin' thing happened today." It's fine, it has to be, I swear like a fuckin' truck driver, but I can still be a lady in a business meeting.

From when the kids were two years old, we told them to shake hands and look people in the eye when they did. People thought it was cute. They were taught to always say please and thank you, and they still use good manners now. Manners cannot be overrated. Being polite is everything—and this applies to swearing, and learning who you can swear in front of, and when.

My kids had to call everybody mister or missus, never could they call an adult by their first name. That still drives me insane. Your kid can call me Mrs. Manzo until I tell them it's OK to call me Caroline. Same goes with swearing. I'll let your kid know when it's OK to drop an f-bomb.

There should be nothing a kid can't tell a parent. If you start breaking a kid because of some of the words they use when they tell you, you're building a wall in your communications that will only get higher and thicker as the kid gets older.

It kills me that a lot of the kids I've met through my own children did not have an open dialogue with their parents, unlike what I shared with my own children. I met kids who told their parents absolutely nothing about their lives, because they were too afraid of their parents' harsh judgment. I was the person they came to with their problems.

Lauren had girlfriends who had problems; they were sexually active and some of them had issues at home. She would tell me that she was going to accompany her friends on doctor visits when they got into trouble. I'd feel awful for her friends, but I'd also be so proud of Lauren for standing by her friends.

My message to those poor kids was always the same. A kid should be able to speak freely in her own home. We told our kids, even if you go out and commit a murder, tell us. No matter what was going on in their lives, we were there to listen. To care. To help. Let your kids tell you about anything at all, let them feel comfortable that you will accept them for who they are and not pick apart every word they say—and learn to listen, and think, before you react. Let them say *fuck*—and maybe you'll help them stay away from the heroin.

Drugs may kill you, but your father will kill you first.

My kids have never experimented with drugs. We scared them straight from very early on. Even though I had kids very young, by that time in my life I had already seen the destruction that pot, coke, and heroin can bring into a family. We had friends and family members with substance problems, and we decided to never hide it from the kids.

One time, when Albie was eight, Lauren was six, and Chris was five, Al lined them all up and said, "If you try drugs, I will kill you. If you put your mother through the pain of dealing with an addict, I will kill you. You do not have a single chance."

I used to show the kids videos of people strung-out and high. When the kids were little we'd drive through the bad parts of Paterson. I'd show them the junkies living on the street and say "This is what drugs do to your life, this is what not working does to your life." And then later when we were at The Brownstone I'd tell them, "This is hard work, this is what Daddy does so you can have a nice life. He works hard. He works long hours. So you can have all the things you have."

The kids knew that drugs weren't recreational. I wanted them to know that using any chemicals at all robbed you of your life, your judgment, and your family.

I have been around drugs my whole life, and they have never interested me. All of my friends smoked pot, from as young as when I was in grammar school. They'd offer it to me, and I'd decline. I didn't care that they were doing it, I just knew it wasn't for me. And I look back on those days and they seem so innocent now—a bit of pot here and there. These days kids are exposed to so much more, and so much worse.

Cocaine, meth, heroin, and speed are not only more available these days, but they're also more affordable. This is perhaps the most terrifying fact of being a parent today. You need to set the ground rules early and stick to them. If you find out, God forbid, that your kids are already using drugs, you only have one option and it's brutal: tough love.

I have a friend whose son got hooked on heroin. After a series of lies and heartbreak, my friend kicked his own son out of the house. The kid went and lived on the streets. And his father, every night, would drive around until he found the doorway that his son was sleeping in. Then he'd park down the street and watch over his son for the whole night. His son was so out of his mind on heroin, he never even knew that his father cared so much that he spent every night in a car, making sure his son was not harmed.

When his son hit rock bottom and asked for help, his father was by his side immediately. They got him into rehab, and they got him clean. The guy has now been sober for years, and he works as a drugs counselor.

When I found out that some of my kids' friends were using drugs, I didn't ban my kids from seeing them, but I made sure they knew never to get in a car with that person if they were high, or to ever go with them when they went to buy drugs.

One time, some of the boys' friends were smoking pot in my driveway when I got home. I lost my temper. I rounded up those kids and read them the riot act. The next day, they came back, apologized, and gave me a sign that read KEEP OFF THE GRASS.

As hilarious as that was, this is one area in which I don't have much of a sense of humor. I'm still terrified of my kids ever touching drugs, but I'm comforted by the fact that my husband will still kill them well before the drugs can.

PART IV

LOVE

Early boyfriends are your training for Mr. Right.

Before meeting Albert, I went on a lot of dates and had three boyfriends. Some of them were more serious than others. The thing is, back then I was pretty shy, so maybe if I was more outgoing I would have been more popular with the boys. Apparently guys would flirt with me, but I was so oblivious for the most part it would sail right over the top of my head. I just didn't pay attention. I was always hearing that guys thought I was a snob for not talking, when the reality was, I was just clueless! When I was a senior in high school, I had my first serious boyfriend, this guy Frankie. He was a baseball player, and he looked just like Rocky Balboa. I was such a good girl, and he was so popular, I had to date him. It's funny now, but to a sixteen-year-old girl, he was irresistible.

Things didn't work out of course. He was older than me, and during the seven months that we dated, he kept wanting to have sex. I knew in my heart that I wasn't ready and I refused. Looking back, it surprises even me that I was able to stand my ground, as I was as gaga in love with him as only a sixteen-year-old girl can be. It wasn't that I was afraid of my parents finding out, or getting into trouble or anything. I just looked in my heart and saw that I was in no way ready to have sex yet.

Frankie was always a gentleman with me, but he clearly wanted us to take things further. He never pressured me, but once it became clear I wasn't going to put out, we split up. The funny thing is, his sister later married my brother, so we became in-laws! He's my niece's uncle, and I see him from time to time at family events. I saw him at her birthday party last year, and my brother pointed at him and joked with me, saying, "Isn't it crazy? If he didn't break up with you, you would have married him!"

I looked at my brother and said, "You're right. I would have married him." You should have seen the shock on my brother's face. It's true. I was so smitten with the guy, if we'd gone all the way and I'd gotten pregnant, we would have gotten married. Would I be as happy as I am now? Most likely not.

Frankie still teases me that he always believed I'd grow up and be a soccer mom and I'd drive one of those station wagons with wood paneling. When I see him these days, I'm always tempted to read him a list of all the nice cars I've driven, the Ferraris and Bentleys and all the rest. I've driven station wagons too, but it makes me happy that he was so wrong about the way I'd turn out.

After Frankie, I dated this guy named Val. It was a lot of fun while it lasted—he was a great-looking guy from a good family. He was a little too privileged, but we dated through the end of high school. His mother was very overprotective and she didn't exactly welcome me with open arms. When during our graduation speech, our school principal singled me out to say that "Caroline Laurita is the picture of integrity," I leaned over to Val and told him to tell his mother what the principal had said.

It didn't matter too much. After about four months of dating, he cheated on me with one of my best friends. I was devastated, and I broke up with him immediately. I heard he wanted me back, but I refused to ever speak to him again. I think he's a dermatologist somewhere in South Carolina, now. I'm sure he's happily married and still a great guy.

After high school, I started getting more moxie when it came to guys. I found it easier and easier to go up to a guy and start talking to him. One day I was at the gym with one of my sisters and I saw this guy working out. He had great legs. We're talking amazing, muscular legs. So I decided to go tell him.

"You have great legs," I said to him.

"Do you think so?" he asked.

"Yeah, I think so, and I think you should take me out," I boldly replied.

He seemed a little surprised, but he asked me out. We had dinner together later that week, and we began dating. His name was Mark, and he was very sweet and kind. I liked him. I don't know that I loved him, though I'm sure I told myself I did at the time. We went on some fun dates and had a lot of laughs together. But everything changed the night I met Al.

Ask Caroline

Dear Caroline, I'm thirty-five and recently divorced after a ten-year marriage. He was my first boyfriend, and I have no dating experience. I grew up in an abusive home, but with the help of counseling have been able to get my life in order. My question is, what are the characteristics of a good, decent man who will love me and cherish me like I deserve?

You've been through a lot, but I'm proud that you've taken control of your life and are moving forward in a positive direction.

A good man will immediately treat you with respect and kindness and accept you as you are. A good man never abuses you, he helps around the house, understands you, and cherishes getting to spend time with you.

True love is a very powerful emotion. When you are deeply connected to someone, you laugh when they laugh, hurt when they hurt. It's easy to have good times together, but the most telling and important signs come during a rough patch. It's how you get through the bad times together that really shows you what kind of man he is.

Good luck. You're thirty-five years young. Prince Charming is out there somewhere.

I fell for Albert at my brother's wedding and broke up with Mark the next day. The poor guy watched me meet Albert, because he was my date at the damn wedding! As soon as he saw us together, he knew it was over for the two of us. He tried to fight for me, but he didn't know how to handle it. I suddenly knew Mark wasn't what I wanted. I wanted a superman.

I'm happy I'd dated the way I did, and in hindsight, I am so grateful that I was cautious with boys. Because when the right guy came along, I was ready.

How to get a guy's attention without looking desperate or cheap

1. Be confident in yourself. Go up and say hello to him. Start a conversation.
2. Dress to reflect yourself. Don't dress like you're on the hunt. Dare to be different.
3. Laugh, and smile, and be engaged when you finally talk to him.
4. Leave a little to the imagination. A business suit can be sexier than a tiny dress.
5. Be clean and polished. Always have your hair neat, your makeup fresh, and your nails and teeth clean.
6. Don't walk up chewing gum with a cigarette hanging out of your mouth.
7. Attitude is everything. When you talk to him, own the conversation. Flirt very subtly. Have fun with him.
8. It's not what you say, it's how you say it. A good conversation can be very seductive, but you have to deliver it well.

I always knew (and wished!) that one day I'd meet that one guy who would blow me off my feet. And I knew that none of the boyfriends before Al were Mr. Right, but I liked them and I was kind to them, and by dating them, I learned a lot about myself and what I wanted in a guy. I'm not saying that everyone has to save themselves for marriage, not at all. I'm just glad I was never a pincushion or a source of locker room conversation. I dated well, and I kept it light. My dating was my training for the longest, most amazing marathon of my life—my marriage to Al.

Picking a man is like picking a racehorse.

I always tell my kids, yes, you need to be physically attracted to who you date, but it's not everything. Beauty fades, and when it does, the ugly comes through. You see the person's soul. It doesn't matter how stunning he is as a young guy, when you have to deal with the soul, you better pray that he has a good one—and they don't always match the exterior.

The Albert I met when I was nineteen was the exact opposite of the guys I'd been attracted to, yet somehow, I knew he was exactly what I wanted for myself and my future. I was immediately able to see his qualities. I saw his dedication to work, I saw the way he loved his family, and as we began to date, I saw the way he was with my younger sisters.

Frannie and Dina were eight and nine when I started dating Albert, and he was amazing with them. He would come to visit me and end up outside playing ball with them. He'd take them to the zoo on his day off. Al was also obsessed with my baby nephew Joe, and he'd scoop that baby up and bounce him on his knee. You could see that he was good with kids, and that he loved kids. The signs that he'd make a great husband were pretty hard to miss.

When it came to me, Albert always treated me like gold. He was so sweet and caring, and somehow, even though he worked very long hours, he always managed to make time for me, to the extent that I felt like I was always seeing him. He must have been exhausted, but he never showed it.

I never imagined I would fall for someone like Al, especially considering how he dressed, but when I got to know him, it became apparent we were meant for each other. Remember, this was 1980 in New Jersey. Al always wore a huge gold medallion, and he accessorized that with a whopping pinkie ring. His hair was permed and he blew it out, and then parted it in the middle. Even for 1980, he was pretty badly dressed. He wasn't unattractive at all, his face and smile were absolutely gorgeous, and he kind of looked like Elvis, but it was the latter, kind of 1970s Elvis. As you can imagine, this was not cool with nineteen-year-old me.

Once I realized that I was actually attracted to this gaudy, decent guy, I told myself, sure, he's all wrong, he's everything I never wanted, but he's perfect for me.

Albert figured out I was the one for him pretty quickly. He'll always say he never thought he'd get a girl like me; in his mind, I was a catch. To me, he was the catch. I say to this day, he's the most beautiful thing I've ever seen.

If you're looking for a long-term relationship, the signs of a good guy are pretty easy to spot. Talk to a guy and see if he's on the same page as you. You're going to need to have the same core values, but you really don't have to agree on everything. You do have to agree on a couple of the important things—whether you both want children, which one of you will work, what values you want to raise the kids with. Make sure he's a listener, and trust your instincts to tell you if he's an honest guy.

Don't stress too much about common interests, I've never considered them to be essential, or too important at all. It's probably healthier if you maintain separate interests. Al's obsessed by technology, golf, hockey, and old westerns. I don't love any of those things. He had season tickets to the hockey for like twenty years, and I'd go with him every now and then, but I didn't give a crap about the game. I just went for the company.

I love to curl up and read. I love to do puzzles. Albert hates to read. But every now and then he'll bring me home a book that he's heard is good, and he'll ask me about what I'm reading.

Ask Caroline

Hi, Caroline. I've been dating a guy for two and a half years, and we've been talking about marriage for at least a year, but he hasn't popped the question yet. Is it time to kick him to the curb, or should I be patient?

This is a tough one. No two relationships are the same, so there's no definitive answer.

The amount of time you've been dating is not reason enough to expect your boyfriend to commit to a life together. You can both talk about it forever, and he may be sincere in his desire to marry you, but it seems like you want it sooner than he does.

I don't know enough about your relationship to answer this, but things like previous relationships, parents' marriage, childhood history, and financial stability all influence people's readiness to get married. He could be struggling with any of these things. Whatever the reason, he's not ready to propose, so it's up to you to decide if you have enough faith to stick around, or if it's indeed time to go. Don't make it an ultimatum. Ask yourself if you're happy, or not, and whether he's worth waiting for. Only you can make that choice.

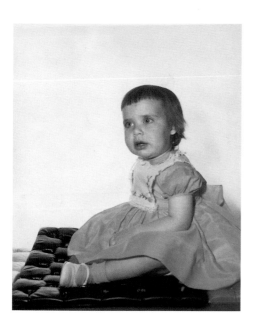

This is me at two years old. Such a baby!

One of my favorite photos of me at school. I thought that butterfly pin was the coolest thing.

I'm about nine years old here—another classic school picture.

Me and my brother Chris at our farmhouse in upstate New York. I'm about ten, and he's six.

Working in my father's office in 1982.
I was twenty-one.

Oh my God. This outfit, this
makeup, this hair. I don't even know
what to say.

Al and me
when we
first started
dating, at
my house in
Kinnelon,
New Jersey.

Albert and me
with Aunt Josie,
his favorite, at
our wedding.
July 7, 1984.

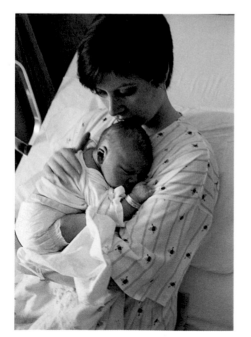

Giving Albie his first bath.
May 1986.

Here I am with Christopher right
after he was born. May 1989,
Wayne General Hospital.

Me with a young Lauren in the front door of our old house in Wayne, New Jersey. She's waving good-bye to her daddy as he goes off to work.

Here is a full family portrait of all five of us on the steps of the house in Wayne. (And yes, Chris is here—he's in my belly!)

I love this shot of all three of my kids. They're four, five, and seven here.

At the front steps of our new home in Franklin Lakes as it was being built.

A vacation snap from a family trip to Boston.

The kids all dressed up in their costumes visiting Al at The Brownstone on Halloween.

I love this pic of me and Albie.
He has such a great smile.

Chris's graduation
from Ramapo High
School. I'm such a
proud mom!

Me and Lauren after Chris's
graduation. We all went into
the city for dinner and ended
up meeting Bill Clinton!

Lauren and I had a ball getting dressed up in our finest English lady's hats for my brother Jamie's wedding in Chicago.

Such a great experience getting the chance to visit the *Rolling Stone* offices with Albie and Christopher.

Me with my mom and dad at a family wedding.

No explanation needed!

Meeting Jay Leno and doing
The Tonight Show was one of
the greatest "pinch myself"
moments of my life.

Albert and I loved visiting Kathy Griffin
backstage at her Broadway show.

Can you believe a fan made this
cake for a *Real Housewives* event that
we did? It was so cool!

The TV show is a great example of how different we are. I was really interested in it when I first auditioned. It sounded like something that would be great fun, and potentially kind of exciting. Albert was not interested in it at all. He said I could do it if I wanted to, so I went and auditioned. When I found out that I had been cast, he did not want to be a part of it, but because it was important to me, he would appear on the show. You'll notice, however, he's not on it as much as the other husbands, and that's at his request. He only does the show because he knows that viewers want to see my entire family life, and he is such a massive part of my life it wouldn't be right if he weren't on the show occasionally. Al also recognizes that for now, this show is my career, and he supports me fully in it.

I've been lucky in love with the man I married, but I've watched my sisters, friends, and my daughter encounter bad guys, and they're thankfully almost as easy to spot. A guy will never be right for you if he doesn't listen to you or respect you. If you meet a guy, and all he wants to do is talk about himself, he doesn't really have time for you or anyone else. Worst of all, if a man belittles you, or makes fun of you or your life, you need to run. A good man is happy to let you have the spotlight and see you shine. Albert and I love to let our lights shine on each other; that's how it should be.

Despite my certainty upon meeting Al, I don't believe in love at first sight. Not at all. When I saw Vito with Lauren, I said, that's going to be your husband. They met when she was sixteen and they didn't even start dating until she was twenty-one. It's first impressions. Who's to say that they'll definitely marry? They've been dating three years, and if you ask me, they're headed that way. It wasn't love at first sight for them, but I immediately recognized that Vito had a lot of the same qualities as Al, and I knew Lauren would come around eventually.

At a very young age, I told myself to find the one who's going to make me smile. I always knew the stereotype of a perfect guy is a myth. However, there's someone out there who's perfect for each of us. You just have to figure out what that is, and be open to it when

Recognize these relationship red flags

If you're not fighting, you're in trouble. Fighting shows you care. If you don't fight, you don't care. I'm talking about little disagreements and spats, they're important.

If he disrespects or talks down to you, it means he has stopped caring for you.

If he belittles or degrades you, this is a big red flag. A need to humiliate you in public is not healthy for you.

If he doesn't take you seriously, it will never work. I'm talking about a man who just says "yes, dear" when you talk about your dreams of the future. He's not treating you as an equal.

If he's emotionally distant, or worse, physically distant, something's wrong. If your husband doesn't want sex, he's getting it from somewhere else.

If your partner has become angry and bitter, something has changed in the way he views you. Try to talk it over to find out what is bothering him before it's too late.

it comes along. I've always said, Al isn't perfect, I'm not perfect, but we're perfectly matched for the longest race of our lives.

Believe in fate.

I believe in fate and God's will, with all my heart. And meeting Al was fate.

My family moved from New York to New Jersey when I was sixteen. I finished school and went right to work. I had no social life at all. I went home from work and cooked and helped my mom. I was dating a guy named Mark, we dated for a year, but somehow I always knew he wasn't going to be the one.

My dad met Al's dad through their attorneys, and they became friends. My brother Anthony was having his wedding at this place in West Orange, and my dad heard that Al's dad had bought The Brownstone, and we should go look at it for the wedding.

My dad went to The Brownstone and he told my brother that he liked The Brownstone and he liked Al's family and he wanted to give them some business. So they moved the wedding to The Brownstone.

Al met my father while he was planning the wedding. I remember my father loved him and came home and told me that he'd love to have a son-in-law like that, a guy who worked hard and was friendly and decent. My dad wanted him to date my sister Ann; she's the same age as Al. I was dating Mark at the time, so Dad didn't even think of Al for me.

One day Al walked into my dad's shop to deliver the place cards for the wedding. I'll never forget it. I was doing the books in my father's office, and I looked up and I saw him, his hair parted in the middle, heavyset, dressed all wrong. Not cool at all. I was used to dating the guidos, the big muscle guys, and I said out loud, "Oh my God." My father's secretary said, "What's wrong?" I said, "I'm going to marry that guy."

I just knew. And it wasn't even that I was attracted to him, I just knew it the second I laid eyes on him. Before we spoke. He was walking down the hallway and I turned my head and saw him walking toward me, the complete opposite of anything I'd ever dated or even looked at. And it hit me like a ton of bricks. We didn't even really talk until my brother's wedding, and I can't explain the feeling in any other way than I just felt certain that this guy was my destiny.

Al's version is so different. He liked my sister. He had heard I was a good girl and he wasn't interested in a good girl. He was only twenty. My sister looked a little wilder, so he was interested in Ann, not me.

It's funny how things happen. My sister Cookie liked his cousin, who was a bartender. And the night before the wedding, we were all out and I made a dare with Cookie that if I could get Al to dance with me at Anthony's wedding the next day, she had to go and talk to his cousin. That's the funny thing, I asked Al to dance so that Cookie could get with his cousin.

So at the wedding—which I went to as Mark's date—I went up to Albert.

"Do you remember me?" I asked.

"Yes, you're Caroline," he said.

"Listen," I said. "I'm the maid of honor tonight and you have to dance with me."

It was the first big wedding The Brownstone had done. He said he couldn't, he was too busy. I refused to take no for an answer. His version of things is that I was wearing a low-cut dress and he could see right down my cleavage, and that's what got his attention.

He says that as soon as he saw my cleavage that was it, he would dance with me.

We danced a slow dance and we got to talking, and poor Mark was there with his parents, realizing he'd lost me, and by this point I didn't give a shit.

Al walked me back to the table because he had to get back to work. And we walked past his parents; they were guests at the wedding too. His dad was a huge bear of a man with a boisterous voice. "Hey you, what are you doing with my son? He's supposed to be working!" he said as we walked by.

I stopped and looked at him—I'd never met this man before in my life—and I said, "I'm gonna marry your son," I said, and I kept walking. I don't know how I knew, but I remember that even then, I was certain. And I can't tell you how happy I am that I followed my instincts—I ended up with my soul mate, and I can't imagine my life without him.

Love can triumph over tragedy.

My engagement was a triumph of love over horrible tragedy. Al and I had been dating for two years. Every day after work, Albert would come pick me up and he'd take me home. We had discussed getting married, and of course, we'd been planning our engagement ring with Al's father. One night after work, I'll never forget, we were driving along Totowa Road, in Paterson, on our way to The Brownstone. As we got to the underpass that goes beneath Route 80, Al suddenly pulled over and parked the car.

I was confused until I saw him fumbling in his pocket and pull out some tissue paper. He unwrapped a gorgeous engagement ring, and held it out to me.

"I love you," he said. "I want you to be my wife!"

I couldn't believe it. I burst into nervous laughter "Are you kidding me?" I replied. I looked around at the dirty underpass and the cars zooming by. This was not exactly where I'd imagined our proposal would take place. And then I looked at his face, and I saw how much he loved me, and I saw that he just couldn't wait one more second to ask me. I burst into hilarious laughter. "Yes, of course, yes," I said. Then I cracked up some more and added, "Is this a joke?" And then we kissed. I was so happy, and my heart was bursting because his love for me was so strong that it had forced him to be so spontaneous, to ask me right there on Totowa Road.

Al's dad bought The Brownstone in 1980 for quite a bit of money. Five months after we got engaged, Al tragically lost his father, in August 1983. They only had the place three years, and with his father's passing Al and his family inherited The Brownstone—and the responsibility to make it work.

In many ways, we were lucky. We had a huge engagement party at The Brownstone before Al's dad passed, and he had the chance to see us so happy. It was a beautiful night, and it became all the more special since he did not live to see our wedding.

For Albert, the loss of his father was the most horrible time, especially considering the tragic way it occurred. We were engaged, and everything in our lives was supposed to be special and romantic and easy. But on August 18 of that year, just four months after we were engaged, Al's father disappeared.

They searched everywhere for the next four days, and found nothing. At 4:00 AM on August 23, which also happened to be my birthday, the doorbell rang. It was the police, and they had found my future father-in-law's body.

Al is the oldest of his siblings. He was twenty-three at the time. He had to go to the police station and be questioned about his own father's death. He was gone all day. I stayed at his house, and people started arriving immediately. When Al finally got home, the house was chaos already. There were people everywhere, there were news crews out front all over the lawn. Literally hundreds of friends and family arrived at the house. But I couldn't find Albert.

I searched everywhere. I asked if anybody had seen him, and nobody had a clue as to where he went. I was worried sick, running all over the place looking for him. He was gone for about an hour and a half. We didn't have cell phones back then, so I was panicked.

When he showed up again, he took me outside to the yard. He led me to a quiet corner, out of sight of everybody, and he put his hands on my face. He looked me in the eyes, with all the hurt and loss on his face, and he said, "Happy birthday."

I was so shocked. I had completely forgotten it was my birthday. It was the last thing on my mind that day.

Albert took me in his arms and gave me a huge hug and a kiss. As he held me, in the middle of all that was going so horribly in his life, he apologized for ruining my birthday. The day they found his father dead, he was concerned about me. And then he gave me the most beautiful ruby and diamond ring. Albert had designed the ring as my birthday gift that year. He had been dropping hints, and I knew that he'd gotten me something cool, but I didn't know what it was. It was a beautiful special ring that he wanted to reflect this amazing time in our lives, and how much I meant to him.

I'll never forget it. We were sitting outside by the pool. My heart burst; I couldn't believe the honor of this man, the man I was engaged to. What kind of guy, at that age, with that horrific thing going on in his life, thinks of somebody else? Albert, that's who.

To this day, the circumstances around what happened to Al's father are a mystery to us, and the years that have passed haven't made it any easier to accept. We spent the rest of our engagement getting stronger and stronger as a couple. The adversity of this time brought us closer together. After it happened, Al told me that he would understand if I didn't want to marry him anymore, but I told him to quit being stupid. Some people told us to postpone our wedding, but we decided to push ahead and stick to our original plan.

That ring that Al gave me for my birthday meant the world to me, and I'm sick to my stomach that I don't have it anymore. My house was robbed just after we were married and it was stolen.

As the years went by, I always teased Al that he never got down on one knee and actually said "will you marry me?" So, as viewers of the show saw, in season three, Al had secretly had my engagement ring redone—same gold, same jewels—and he took me back to that Route 80 underpass. He pulled over, and this time, he got out of the car. As soon as he got down on one knee, I knew what he was up to, and I burst out laughing, exactly the same way I did the first time.

I remembered the clumsy kid in jeans and a short-sleeved plaid shirt who had nervously proposed to me thirty years ago, and then I looked at the handsome, well-dressed, successful man on his knee thirty years later, still loving me just as much. It was probably the best feeling in the world. And Al said the magic words. For that moment, that dirty underpass became the most romantic place on earth, for the second time in my life.

Don't become a Bridezilla!

I never lost my mind as a potential bride. I loved being engaged and I loved planning a wedding, but I was never obsessed with any of the details. In fact, I wanted it all to be simple and modest. My father-in-law couldn't get over how I acted when we were choosing an engagement ring. He had a friend who was a jeweler, and he'd come home with all these diamonds, wrapped in tissue paper, for me to look at.

They were huge. Some of them would come up to my knuckles. He would show them to me, hoping I'd choose one. And I'd just shake my head. He'd be so shocked; he would tell me that any girl in the world would die to have a ring with such a large diamond. I'd just keep shaking my head.

I'm a tiny woman. A huge diamond would look stupid on my hand. One time, after I had rejected an entire bag of absolutely gorgeous, huge diamonds, my father-in-law got so angry he snatched them off the table and shoved them into his pocket. He stormed over to Albert and told him he wouldn't bring any more diamonds home for me.

"Good," Albert said. "I'll get my own ring." Albert knew what I wanted, and he went and got me the exact perfect ring.

That set the tone for my approach to the whole wedding. I knew that people I loved could be trusted to do things the way I liked. We were engaged in April, and after we dealt with the loss of Albert's father that August, we decided to not change our wedding date for the following July.

I was never a Bridezilla. That wasn't how I wanted to approach my own wedding. I wanted to be carefree—well, almost. I kept myself

Ask Caroline

Caroline, I need your help! My fiancé and I have been engaged for two years and we've saved enough for our wedding. We've set a budget of fifteen grand, which is modest, but we are also saving up for our first home. My problem is, there are a lot of family weddings, and things are getting competitive. Do we stick with the modest wedding and get ahead on our first home, or do a bigger, more memorable wedding? His family is pushing for the lavish wedding. Mine doesn't care. I'm starting to hate planning the wedding. What should I do?

You sound miserable, and I'm sorry. You have your head on straight and your priorities in order. Spending more money on a wedding doesn't make it better or more memorable. Trying to buy the approval of others is pointless, and so is trying to compete with other weddings.

If your future in-laws want to contribute some cash to make the wedding more lavish, then fine, let them. If not, they'll have to deal with your simple, beautiful, modest wedding.

Every girl dreams of the perfect wedding, and maybe you won't have all the silly bells and whistles at your wedding, but at the end of the day, you'll have a husband waiting for you with keys to your new home in his pocket, and that's priceless.

involved in the planning, but we had never done a big, crazy wedding in my family at that time. My oldest sister had eloped, and the next sister had married so quickly we didn't have much time to plan anything special. My brother had had a big wedding, but we didn't really plan it. We consciously downsized our wedding due to what had happened to Al's father. If he had still been alive, we would have had six hundred people at our wedding. As it was, we had three hundred, and I managed it without a single screaming fit or headache.

Everyone around me helped make my day special. Albert asked what I wanted for our wedding meal. "It's our wedding and I want meat loaf," I told him. He was surprised, but he knew I was just joking to make a point about how little I cared about details like that. I was pleased when the menu for the wedding was veal rollatini and fish. That worked just as well as anything I could have spent hours agonizing over.

I went to buy my gown with my mom and my dad, and I chose the first gown I tried on. I fell in love with it the minute I laid eyes on it—it was a Sposabella gown from Italy. There were two versions, one with sequins, one without sequins. The version with the sequins was double the price. My mother and I looked at each other, knowing how crazy it would be to buy the one double in price, so we bought the plain one and put the sequins on ourselves.

I have such great memories of the night before my wedding, my mom and all my sisters and my sister-in-law, all sitting around, putting the sequins on that dress. We laughed and talked and beaded my entire wedding gown.

My mom made silk flower arrangements, and I let her do whatever she thought would look good for the floral centerpieces. And she did—it looked great. I didn't worry about a single thing and it all worked out perfectly.

If you just got engaged, or when you do, remember that nothing else matters on that day as long as you are happy. A wedding needs to be fun, and it needs to be about love. You can have a great wedding using paper towels for napkins and plastic tablecloths if the room is full of love.

The problem now is that a lot of women are losing sight of what a wedding is. A wedding is a wonderful party; it's a time for a woman to shine and have the moment she's dreamed of all her life. But at its core, a wedding is two people coming together to begin a shared life. I've seen so many kids waste hundreds of thousands of dollars of their parents' money on stupid things like flowers that cost ten thousand dollars and will be dead in two days, or two thousand dollars on linen tablecloths that will never be used again. Guess what? People go home and say they went to a great wedding if people were laughing and dancing all night. Nobody has ever said a wedding was great because the tablecloths were awesome.

I was calm all the way right up to my wedding. Honestly nothing mattered, and I knew the thing I wanted out of that day was to become Albert's wife. Everything else was unimportant. I even let my

Tips to plan a perfect wedding

Consciously avoid stress. Enjoy the day. Don't get caught up in the event so much that you forget about why you're there in the first place Hire people with experience to take care of the details, or let friends help out.

Enjoy your guests. Take time to sit and chat with each of them.

Anything except a natural disaster is fine. If it rains or snows on your wedding day, that's all just part of what makes your wedding day unique.

Don't micromanage your wedding day. Let the day unfold as it is meant to. It will never be what you think it will be, but it's your wedding whatever happens. Relax and enjoy the ride.

Take time to be with your husband. You'll both be pulled in a million directions, but it's your day. And when you sit to eat, actually eat your food!

mother-in-law plan our honeymoon. She suggested San Francisco and Hawaii, and we said, sure sounds good, book it. I just didn't care about anything. I was the furthest thing from a Bridezilla on the planet.

The only thing that has to be perfect on your wedding day is your love for each other. A good wedding needs three things: Good food, good music, and lots of love. If you have those three things, nothing else matters.

Marriage is a marathon; you gotta stay in shape!

My children have been my priority since I became a mother, but I've always made sure to be a wife first and Mommy second. My marriage is the foundation that supports my whole life, and I have always been conscious of keeping it healthy.

The secret to a long marriage is in the details. Always take the time to be thoughtful, always take time to make sure that your partner feels loved, appreciated, and special. If you do that, then it's easy.

The details are small, and they mean the world. Al has to take a bunch of pills every day, for blood pressure and whatnot. And every night before I go to bed, I lay out his pills, and I put a little handwritten note for him to see in the morning. The note will say something along the lines of "please take these pills, I love you and I like having you around!" And when he sees the note, he can smile and know how much he means to me.

It's crazy to me when I look at photos of us when we started dating. I see two kids who had not much of a clue what they were doing. And then I think of him and me these days, how embedded we are in each other's soul. We've been through the best of times together and the worst of times. And we're still here.

LOVE

I used to love running my fingers through his hair. I could lay in bed for hours and just run my fingers through his hair and be content. Thirty years later, he's bald, and now my favorite part of his body is this tuft of hair on his chest. I run my fingers through that now, and it makes me just as happy.

It's the stupid things like that that keep a marriage fresh. We say silly, parochial things to each other, it's almost corny. But we communicate. If I'm cold, I'll put on one of his coats and smell his cologne and I'll always call him and tell him that I smelled his cologne and it made me smile.

You don't have to give someone a box of chocolates or a bunch of flowers, you just have to let them know you love them every time you talk. We've probably never ended a phone call to each other without saying "I love you."

The place where Al and I are now did not happen overnight. This place in our relationship was thirty years in the making. We were romantic and dating at first and then life got in the way. Al's father's murder and then back-to-back kids made for a difficult period in our lives, but they made us stronger. It was tough to make time for each other when we had the kids, but we did whenever we could. We came up with a perfect solution—I'd have a sitter come over at midnight, while the kids were sleeping. Al would come get me at around 2:00 AM when he was finished with work, and we'd head into New York City. We'd go to Blue Ribbon, I love it there, and it's open until 4:00 AM. I knew I'd be exhausted the next day, but this was our time to be romantic. This was when he'd hold my hand and we would just be that same couple that fell in love years earlier.

I see a long relationship as a house that you're building. And every event that happens to you as a couple is another brick in the wall of your house. And every event that you get through together is another layer. So when you've just started dating, your house is still being built. You have the foundation and one brick. It's not a house yet. You have to stay together and be patient, and let the bricks start to add up, until you have built a very strong house that can withstand anything.

When you're young and still in the beginning or honeymoon stage of dating, your relationship is just a baby. You're still going to dinners and seeing movies and going on great vacations. You'll need to come through some bad times together before you get stronger.

The absolute essential thing that is a good foundation for a long marriage is your friendship with your partner. You can never become boring to him and have to keep up with him. If your husband loves football, sports of any kind, develop at least a basic knowledge of it so he can talk to you. Just the same for him—he needs to know about whatever your hobbies are outside of him. Also never ever become a nag. No man wants to be married to his mother. Nags are awful people. Nagging gets you nowhere.

I love the way Albert looks today. There are things I love about him now that I didn't see then. He's a man now. He was a boy then. When I look at him, he's still the boy I started dating. He says when he looks at me, he can still see the little square-faced girl that he met thirty-one years ago.

I cannot wait for the next phase in our lives, when we become grandparents. He and I talk about it all the time. We talk about selling our house when the kids move out, but we need something that is still big enough for our grandkids to come stay. We talk about getting a place by Central Park so we can take the kids into the park all the time, or maybe even out on Cape Cod, or Hoboken, so we can have a boat.

Albert will be an incredible grandfather, and I feel like the next thirty years will be even better than the first. He'll be retiring soon, hopefully, and we're really going to travel the world together and do all the stuff he never got to do because he dedicated his life to making our life better. Now I want to pay him back.

I'm thrilled to think of myself at eighty, married to Al for sixty years and surrounded by grandkids. After getting our marriage into great shape for thirty years, I think the next thirty will be a snap.

I'll look at Al when he's eighty, and I'll still be saying, there's my handsome man. I'll hold his hands, look into his eyes, and know that he's in every fiber of me.

Ask Caroline

Caroline: I recently got married and had a baby. I'm currently on maternity leave, and my husband and I are still financially separate. Despite having some savings, I know that soon I will have to rely on my husband financially, but I have been independent for so long that I'm worried I'll feel like a kept woman. How do I address this with my husband?

I think it's great that you want to maintain a sense of independence, but you have to realize that the landscape of your life has changed. It's OK to have separate bank and checking accounts as a married couple, but there comes a time when you have to realize that a marriage is a partnership, and when children come into the picture the game changes.

There is absolutely no shame in relying on your husband; it's his child too.

You are certainly not a kept woman, your role in life has shifted, and you have a responsibility to your child now, that's why they call you Mommy and Daddy.

As far as feeling like a kept woman, let me know how you feel a couple of months from now; a mother's work is the most grueling work on the planet. You have no sick days, no time off, and no overtime pay. A kept woman? Hardly . . . the reward is *priceless* and so worth the sacrifice.

Marrying someone I never lived with was tough—and so were our early years.

It all seems so old-fashioned now, but when we got married, we had never lived together. We'd never been away together. So after the whirlwind of our wedding day, we flew off to San Francisco to begin our honeymoon, and it was such a huge adjustment, we both freaked-out!

The morning after we arrived, we woke up in bed and just stared at each other, not speaking at all. Albert finally broke the silence and said what was on both our minds: "Did we make a mistake?"

I looked into his eyes, and I was just so confused.

"You know, I think we did," I said. "I think I want to go home."

We lay in bed a long time, and we started talking. We realized that we were both just so damned nervous. It felt like there was so much weight on our shoulders, and at that moment we felt like complete strangers. We both wanted to run home to our old lives!

We agreed to stay on the honeymoon, to have as much fun as we could, and if things didn't work out, we'd go home and break up. We'd give back all the presents and go our separate ways.

The next day we woke up laughing, realizing what stupid idiots we were. We just had the worst case of jitters, of stepping into a new life and realizing that everything we'd known our whole lives was now completely changed. We went on to have such a beautiful, memorable honeymoon, and then we returned to New Jersey to start our new life, and once again, I had a lot of learning to do.

I had a lot to adjust to. I had lived in a house that was always full of people; I have never liked being home alone. Suddenly, I was home, alone, a lot. It was my worst nightmare, and I had to figure out how to deal with it. We lived above The Brownstone, so if Al had a free moment, he'd sneak upstairs to see me. Sometimes, I'd go down and work with him, just so we had some time together.

Ask Caroline

Caroline, my husband is a very busy physician and he works at least eighty hours a week. I don't see this changing anytime soon. While I'm grateful for all his hard work, I often feel lonely and disconnected. We have one young son, and we live two thousand miles from where we grew up, and our families. Any suggestions?

I know the feeling. My husband works long hours as well, but this is something I knew and accepted as part of our relationship from the beginning. I would imagine the same holds true for a doctor's wife.

I'd suggest that you have a conversation with your husband and try to find a balance between his home and work life. It's important that you both get onto the same page, which will take a bit of compromise from both sides.

If your husband is making an effort to spend time with you at home, then find ways to make these moments special. Be affectionate to him, and let your son see that you love each other.

When your husband is working, take a minute to text him that you love him, or send him a picture of you and your son waving to him. Leave a lipstick kiss on the mirror for him to see when he comes home late. Small gestures go a long way.

Even though your families are far away, you are surrounded by people who can become good friends. Find something that interests you. Join a gym, volunteer at a hospital, take classes at a local college, anything. Just do something. Do not sit around and feel sorry for yourself.

Trust me, I've been in your shoes, and in many ways I still am. Attitude is everything. If you have a good man and your relationship is solid, you will find a way to make it work.

Al had to make the business work. He was taking care of his family and me. Sometimes it just got to be too much for the both of us. To me, it felt like there was never time for us as a couple. He was working seven days a week, from noon until three in the morning. I would bombard him with demands, that I needed more of his time. I needed to know when we'd have time to make us work as a couple.

I'd break down and then I'd regroup. I'd realize that I was being unreasonable. People asked how I dealt with Al's long hours, and my answer was always that it wasn't like he was at the golf course, he was at work. He was missing out on doing things he wanted to do too.

I won't lie. Sometimes I'd just fall apart. I'd cry. I would think I couldn't do it anymore. We had no money; we lived in an apartment above The Brownstone after we got married. We showed it last season on the TV show, when we went back there for our anniversary. When I go there these days, I smile from ear to ear. I remember our time in that apartment, and I look at how far we've come. But at the time he was making $200 a week, and working 105 hours a week for the paycheck.

We lived in that apartment for two years, until Albie was born. Then we were lucky enough to be able to afford a house when Albie was four months old.

I had three kids in three years. When I found out I was pregnant with Christopher, Lauren was only four months old, and I just had a complete breakdown. It just didn't seem fair. When I found out that I was going to be dealing with three kids under three, it just all hit me at once.

When I brought Christopher home on Albie's third birthday, I was alone. My mother-in-law was a tremendous help—I'd go by her house all day with the kids and hang out, but at seven o'clock I'd go back to my house, and I'd be alone with the kids until Albert got home seven or eight hours later.

There was a short period after Christopher's birth when I stopped caring about what I looked like. It was too hard. I was full of self-pity, and Al was never home, so I just said to myself, "Why did I even have to bother to try?"

My mother stepped in. She told me I was young and beautiful and

How to make time for date nights when you have kids

1. Go with what works for you. If your husband works nights, have a breakfast date. Use whatever time you have. You'll be surprised how romantic this can be.

2. Meet in the kitchen for coffee every morning before the kids wake up, and talk about whatever's on your mind.

3. A date doesn't have to be a big-budget special event. It can be a shared moment at any time of the day. Sometimes I like to go hug Al while he's shaving, and we laugh and catch up and it's as good as any date we've been on.

4. Time to connect is more important than insisting on the pressure of a full date night. If you are both too busy to plan a big date, try to ensure that you have a half hour to yourselves each day to just check in with each other.

5. Call and say I love you, or send a text. Do it whenever he pops into your mind, so you are letting him know that you're thinking of him.

6. A movie isn't date night. That's not connecting. I mean, if you want to go see a movie, fine, but it doesn't count as date night.

7. Find a great sitter that you and your kids both like, and treat him or her very well.

my husband deserved to see his young beautiful wife every day—even if he only saw me for five minutes!

When I was younger and less secure, I worried about other women. People meet Albert at The Brownstone and assume he's rich. It's always a party atmosphere in that place, and I'd seen a lot of women flirting with my husband. Some days, I'd lie in bed and worry that he wasn't really at work, that he was with another woman somewhere.

Ultimately it was the kids, and not me, that got Albert to work a little less. They were very small, but they were all having those breakthrough moments, almost every day. Those little firsts that are so wonderful—first steps, first words—and Albert was missing them all. I told him that he needed to take time and be present for these milestones. It wasn't just him and me anymore, he needed to make the time to be with these kids. So we created Daddy Day. It's Wednesday. We go to dinner with our kids, even now at least one of them, every Wednesday. And on that day, he dedicates himself to me and the family.

I'm still not a perfect wife. I'm somewhere between a good wife and an excellent one. Albert made a smart choice when he married me, and I work my ass off to make sure it's still a smart choice. We grew up together, and we went through hell and back together. I had two miscarriages, we lost his father, his business was a struggle, but we literally worked so closely together that we made it through it all and became great for each other. And I learned that it's better to be an understanding wife than a perfect wife.

My miscarriages didn't destroy me.

I had two miscarriages when I was very young. My first pregnancy ended in a miscarriage, and I had another one in between

Albie and Lauren. The first one was terrifying for me. I was upset and I was so scared. We had been so happy to discover that we were going to have a baby, and then we learned that there was something wrong the week of my sister-in-law's wedding, and I was in the bridal party.

I remember feeling unwell, but I couldn't put my finger on it. Then I started cramping and staining. Al called the doctor, and he came and examined me. He told me the baby still had a heartbeat, and I was to stay on my back to try to keep the baby healthy. On the night before Al's sister's wedding, I went to the hospital for another examination, and the doctor told me that the heartbeat was gone,

The doctor told me that I had lost the baby, and I needed to walk in order to bring on a miscarriage. They were going to make me walk the halls of that hospital until my body miscarried naturally, and they told me that it could take hours of walking to make that happen.

I looked at Albert and told him I wanted him to go home. I wanted him to leave, and I wanted him to be at his sister's wedding the next day. Their father was gone, his family needed him. He argued, he wanted to stay, but I stood firm. There was nothing he could do for me at that point except stare at me. I wanted him to go.

He eventually left, and I cried my ass off. When I was done crying, I got up and I just walked and walked all night until it happened. It was all so awful, and such a blur. To this day, I'm happy I made Al leave, and I'm happy that he got to be there for his sister at her wedding, even though it was not an easy day for any of us.

The second miscarriage was worse in that I already had one happy, healthy baby, I knew the joy of having a successful pregnancy, and I also remembered the horrible experience of losing a baby. I knew what I was in for, and that didn't make it any easier.

The second time, they made me do the walking too. And once again, I told Al to leave.

He really fought me that time. He was determined to stay. I began the walking with him by my side, but after a while, I forced him to leave. I knew what was ahead of me, and I didn't want him to see it happen. I didn't want him to have to think about what was happening, and I didn't want to look into his eyes when it happened.

Al left and went back to work at The Brownstone. I walked for several hours, and once it was time for the D and C, he came back and was with me for that part. It was just a sad, grim time for us both.

Throughout these miscarriages, I managed to hold it together. Both times I was very matter-of-fact about it. I told myself, *It's not what God wants.* I knew that I just wasn't meant to have that baby. Maybe there was something wrong with that baby, and maybe I was dodging a bullet.

I never grieved at all. I was almost cold about it. But both of those pregnancies ended early. I never felt those babies kick, I never knew if they were boys or girls, I never felt that little flutter that tells you that there's a life growing inside you. My sadness around those times was me grieving about the thought of being pregnant.

God bless these poor women who carry to full term or have to give birth to a baby that they've lost. I can barely imagine going through that, and I praise the Lord that I've never had to experience it. I could never underestimate the agony that someone would feel after going through that. It's a huge difference; I miscarried at eight or ten weeks, both times. They were babies that just weren't meant to be.

When I got pregnant with each of my kids, I was scared. I could never look forward to pregnancy, I was always terrified of miscarrying. The fear got even worse after I'd felt that first little flutter and I knew something was moving around inside me. It was just so hard to be confident that I'd carry the baby to term, that it wouldn't end in heartbreak. But three times, I was lucky.

When people ask how many children I have, I tell them I have three. I know I'll meet the other two in heaven one day. Christopher, Lauren, and Albie are the three kids I was meant to have. I can't imagine my life without them.

Ask Caroline

Caroline! I watch the show while I'm feeding my one-month-old. We only have one child now but we want more. What can we do to make sure our kids are as close as yours are? My husband wants to have number two right away, but I want to wait—what age difference is good?

I don't think the age difference matters. That's up to you and your husband, talking and deciding when you are both ready to add another child.

As for keeping the children close, I think that had a lot to do with Albert and I being very hands-on with our kids. We took family vacations together, and we took the kids to watch each other's sports games. We would get the kids to help each other with homework and chores around the house. We would all sit and talk and laugh at the dinner table. When they argued or fought, we'd try to let them sort it out, and they learned how to communicate and how to forgive. Never favor one of your kids over the others, and they'll never resent each other.

Good luck! Give your baby a hug from me.

For a stay-at-home mom, I've had some crazy adventures.

I'm not adventurous, but I'll always go with the flow. As a wife, as a mother, I've been happy to stay at home. But this hasn't prevented me from having some wonderful adventures.

I've been to Italy twice, Jordan and Dubai once, but most of our lives, our trips have been inside the United States with our kids. The full-on "rent an RV and see the sights" kind of tour.

We've been to Vegas, Utah, Disney World, all the places that kids want their parents to take them. As boring as it might sound, I've had some incredible times showing my kids the United States.

We were on an RV trip through Utah with Chris and Jacqueline and we saw a little hut that sold bison burgers. All the kids started yelling about how they wanted to try a bison burger, so we pulled in to this little diner. And after we ate, we saw a sign that said HORSE-BACK RIDES. So the kids started wanting to go ride horses.

We all were already dirty and messy from living in the RV, so we just suited up and got onto these horses, and it turned into one of my favorite experiences of my life.

It turned out we were a lot closer to the Grand Canyon than we thought we were, and we could have ridden down into the canyon if we wanted to. I was too scared of the heights, so we rode along the top rim.

We were riding along in a group and after a while the land around us opened up and you could just really ride your horse, like you were in a western. Everybody was racing all over on their horses, chasing each other over hills. We were riding them really hard and laughing and then all of a sudden we came upon a herd of buffalo, and we had to ride our horses right through the middle of them all. It really felt like, just because we'd stopped for a stupid burger, that now I was in the middle of the Wild Wild West and my kids were

My top ten world destinations when we retire

I've seen a lot of America but I'm excited to become a globe-trotter when Al retires from The Brownstone. We will need to be gone a lot to cover this much ground:

1. **Paris:** I've never been and it's a goal. I don't know why it's taken so long. I'm sure I'll love it.

2. **Monte Carlo:** I want to go to the races. I love watching them on TV but I think the energy would be amazing to experience in person. And I hear it's beautiful there.

3. **Ireland and Scotland:** I want to see medieval castles. I'm fascinated by that era and think it will be magical to explore such an old culture.

4. **Australia:** I want to go and see the beautiful beaches, and explore the outback.

5. **An African safari:** It's been a dream of mine for years, but this will be one trip we definitely take all the kids on.

6. **Sweden:** I grew fascinated with Sweden while reading *The Girl with the Dragon Tattoo* and would love to go and see it for myself.

7. **Alaska:** I want to do a cruise where we sail around the glaciers and the icebergs and explore the frontier. I want to see the Northern Lights too.

8. **London:** I can't believe I've never been. It's almost embarrassing.

9. **Bali:** I've always been intrigued by Bali. Maybe we'll have a beach getaway soon . . . I need one.

10. **Egypt:** I need to see the pyramids.

Are we there yet?

People think they have to be high-tech when it comes to keeping kids happy on a long drive. Wrong! It's the stupid little games that you play with your kids that they remember and cherish. You don't need to go out and buy an iPad . . . just be creative and teach them the games you loved when you were a kid.

Coloring books, crayons, and crossword puzzles. Stock up on a bunch of coloring and puzzle books, plus Mad Libs, and everyone will be laughing the whole drive.

"I Spy" is the best game ever. You can play this one for hours.

The license plate game. There are so many variations. We used to race to be the first one to see plates from ten different states.

The alphabet game. You have to think of an animal that starts with a letter, and when someone guesses, you take the last letter of that animal's name and then that's the letter that the next person has to use to guess an animal. For example, I would say "K." Lauren would say "kangaroo," so the next person would have to guess an animal whose name started with O. When someone says an animal that's already been used, they're out.

A staring contest or a no-laughing contest can be so hilarious. I like the no-laughing contest, because it's crazy how fun it can be to have your family trying to crack someone up.

having an experience that they'd remember for their whole lives. It was a simple, magical time.

BEHIND THE SCENES

We nearly froze to death when we went to film in Italy. It felt even colder than the brutal Jersey winter we'd left behind. They had us on such a tight schedule that we literally weren't even allowed to stop for coffee. One morning I had to film some scenes, and by the time I was done, the crew of the ship told me that I had missed breakfast and there wouldn't be any more food or coffee until 2 P.M. I was hungry and I really needed a coffee. I said, show me where the captain gets his coffee, because I'm not getting off this boat without a coffee in my hand. They found me a coffee. We were kept so busy in Venice that we could not stop and look at anything. It was insane to have to walk by all these amazing buildings and stylish stores, and not be allowed to stop and go inside. Luckily I'd been to Venice six months before then, so that made it a little better. A little . . .

Al and I have been friends with Bernie Kerik, the former police commissioner of New York, for years. After he retired, he used to travel to Jordan all the time for work. I would watch Al's face as he listened to Bernie's stories about being in Jordan; he was just fascinated because he's such a history buff. So one day, I said to Bernie, next time you get your tickets, buy one for Al and take him with you—and for Christmas that year, I gave Albert a trip to Jordan.

Albert lasted about two days without me in Jordan before he called and said, pack your bags, we want you and Bernie's wife, Hala, here with us. He shot the gift right back at me; he wanted me to see this with him.

It was a truly amazing time. Through Bernie we got to hang out with the royal family, and we visited Petra and many religious sites. It was literally breathtaking to see these things I'd read about my whole life, things that almost don't seem real until you see them. There was so much history in Jordan, I would love to go back.

We stopped in Dubai on the way to Jordan, but I didn't care too much for it. I remember waking up in the morning and seeing

My favorite places in the world

Cape Cod. It's so peaceful and beautiful. Everything about it is pleasant, and I hope we retire to a house on the sea on Cape Cod one day.

Tuscany, in Italy. The rolling hills, just covered in acres of sunflowers as far as the eye can see. Amazing!

Petra, in Jordan. This is a magnificent place. We walked along the stone path that Moses walked on; the actual stones are still there. It's mind-blowing to walk that path and know that Moses's feet touched the same stones as your feet. If you've never been you have to go.

New York City. There's nothing better than being on a boat on the Hudson River at sunset when all the lights are starting to come on and the city is shimmering. To see the Statue of Liberty at dusk with the torch lit, with the City sparkling next to it, takes your breath away. I never get sick of seeing it.

Carmel, California. That drive along Highway 1 down the coast from Carmel to Big Sur is incredible. It's terrifying, with steep cliffs on the side of the road, but it's so gorgeous. It's beautifully terrifying. You think you're going to fall off a cliff.

people sweeping the highways. It was so immaculate that the whole country felt like Disney World, like a facade that wasn't real.

So apart from a trip to Italy for our twenty-fifth anniversary, I was pretty much a local traveler. I was always up for theme parks with the kids. I used to love roller coasters, or any ride that went fast and scared the crap out of me. The crazier the ride, the happier I was. I was pissed to discover that as you get older, these rides cease to be fun because they just give you headaches. After a while, I became the parent who sat with the kids who were too short to go on a ride. Once Albert put lifts in Chris's shoes before we went to Six Flags here in Jersey because he was so close to being tall enough. I couldn't believe it; I didn't want him to do it. But Al put the lifts in, and Chris was able to ride all the roller coasters with his brother, and he loved it.

To this day, I love to go on the teacup ride with Al, he will spin the wheel so fast and it makes the kids laugh so hard to see me screaming like that at their father.

I feel that now, in our lives, the real adventures are about to begin. Albert and I have the world at our feet, and I can't wait to get out and see it. I thought that it would be fine to go to countries where *Housewives* isn't shown, but I hadn't thought about other travelers! When we were in Italy for our twenty-fifth anniversary, we ended up getting chased by American tourists. It was ridiculous, being chased down the piazzas. I know the show is big in England and Australia and Germany, so I guess I'll wait to go to those places.

BEHIND THE SCENES

There was a massive storm in Jersey on the day we were due to depart for our trip to California in season four. The governor closed the airport the night before we were due to board our plane. Production found us a flight out of Pittsburgh and rented us a fleet of black SUVs so that we could all drive ourselves to Pittsburgh. I got furious—why couldn't we just rent a private jet out of nearby Teterboro airport? No dice. They made us drive six hours in a storm, then we had to wait three hours for a flight to Austin, Texas. Then we waited three more hours in Austin before we were able to fly to San Francisco. If you wonder why tempers frayed on that trip, look at how it started!

Our next trip, I hope, will be to Scotland and Ireland, to explore all the old castles and ruins and see the gorgeous countryside. Then I want to go back to Italy, and do a foodie tour. I want to see Paris and London. We also want to buy a boat and spend our summers sailing up and down the East Coast. Years ago, we used to take the kids to Cape Cod, to a town called Orleans. I want a house there, but now we're worried about living too far away from our future grandkids.

It doesn't matter to me that I may not speak the language in the countries I want to go to, or know my way around or understand their customs. I've waited my whole life to see this planet of ours, and now that Al is about to have the time, I can't wait for the best job a retiree can have: tour guide!

Cheating? It didn't happen, but it could.

I've had plenty of opportunities to cheat on Al. Over the years a lot of men have come up to me, they've pinched my ass, they've flirted, they've propositioned me. I've always laughed them off, shrugged them away. Why the hell would I ever cheat? Why would I risk what I have at home for a few hours of fun?

Traveling in an RV with the Housewives: fun or not?

I was not looking forward to our trip to California for the show. I was already unhappy with the way things were going that season and just did not want to spend a week in an RV. I was lucky because they put us in an RV with the Lauritas. That meant that when the cameras weren't rolling I got a vacation with my family and my brother's family, and I actually enjoyed those times a lot. Beyond that I was miserable for the entire time. Everybody else was just worried about playing a game that I wanted no part of. There was so much pressure and tension, every time I walked out of the RV, I got a chill in my heart. Albert and I fought a lot because I couldn't snap out of it. It wasn't all bad, of course. One night we actually had fun when everyone let their guard down around the campfire. But for the most part, what you see on that trip is me at my unhappiest. I hope that they never make us do anything like that again!

I've worked for too many years to throw it away on a fling. Men have tried for years, and the answer is now and will always be no. I'm fiercely loyal to Albert, and I'm just as committed. Nothing is worth losing a lifetime with somebody else. What do you get out of an affair? Do you get to check it out with someone else? Is it even that interesting? I'll tell you what—it's not interesting enough to risk your marriage.

But I think that times have changed and now people use the term "hook up" very lightly. Men and women seem to be much better at separating sex from feelings. They can have sex with no strings attached, they can almost do it for fun. Of course, some people do fall in love with their affairs, and that scenario is never going to end well. These days, it seems people can hook up recreationally and move on without a second thought. They can pick up a stranger in a bar, bang them, and come home without ever thinking of that person again. People can do whatever the hell they like, but I am definitely not wired this way.

There are many types of cheater. There's the guy who makes a mistake just one time, and there are serial cheaters. How you react depends on your situation. The worst thing you can ever do is confront your partner with both guns a-blazing.

If you think your partner has cheated on you, before you even confront your partner, try to learn the specifics of the situation. And then ask yourself, why did he cheat? Is there something broken in your relationship? When I hear that a guy is cheating, I always wonder if his wife stopped giving him attention, or if she became so involved in her kids' lives that she has forgotten about him altogether.

I hear about people who cheat on their partners because they don't like it that the partner has gained weight. They're assholes. Love is blind, and beauty is in the eye of the beholder. If a person is still attentive to their mate, they won't care that they gained weight for whatever reason. When I see Albert, I don't see a bald man with a gray beard. I see the man I fell in love with.

If you ask yourself what's broken and the answer is that your relationship is in trouble, you sit down and talk it out. You loved each other enough to get married, where's that love now? If the following words are coming out of your mouth on a regular basis—"Where are you going? Are you going out with your friends again? When are you going to fix the roof? You need to pick up the lawn!"—then you've turned into your mother. Shut the hell up and be his friend. Guess what? He didn't marry his mother, he married his girlfriend. Fix your marriage and work through the momentary indiscretion.

I don't know if Al has ever cheated. I don't have any reason to suspect that he's ever cheated. But I do know that the odds are against me. I'm certainly not going to open up Pandora's box and ask if at some point during the last thirty years, he messed around on me. If he did, it would have been in a moment of weakness or at a time when he was stressed. I honestly don't know. I'm making assumptions here. But statistically speaking, he was twenty when we met, and we dated from that young age. All logic tells me that the odds are stacked wildly against me. And I'm fine with it because there's never been any indication of any other relationship from him. I'm just saying that my brain tells me that the odds aren't in my favor.

Listen, if he'd come home with lipstick on his collar, I would want to know what the hell was going on. I've never seen lipstick or smelled another woman's perfume on my husband. I don't see the point in going looking for something that's not necessarily there.

My husband would die for me, he'd take a bullet for me. So why would I want to go back in time and say, wait a minute, did you have a fling? No, I'm not going to do that. I understand that I married this man at a very young age. He dealt with tremendous pressure and responsibility. And if he fell or stumbled, he picked himself up. I'm not going to obsess over it, but I'm aware of the realities of my situation.

How to argue with your husband so he still loves you!

Everyone argues. It's a fact of life. When it comes to my marriage, I always argue with a smile on my face. In the middle of an argument I'll ask "What's the problem, let's talk about it," we'll break it down, and then I'll laugh, realizing that there's really no need for an argument after all. Very little is worth having a war over, so I'll start to crack a joke rather than crack a skull.

Al and I don't fight much, but we disagree all the time. In thirty years, we've maybe had four major fights but a million disagreements. I'm smart enough to see that moment when something can turn into a war if I choose to be an asshole. At that point, I lighten the mood and make a joke. "You're gonna leave me now? You gonna draw up divorce papers?" It defuses the argument very effectively.

It makes you realize that whatever you're arguing about isn't as important as being happy with each other.

Last season on the show during the episode where it was our anniversary, we went to our old apartment above The Brownstone and Al got strawberries and champagne. There was no way I was going to give the producers footage of me eating strawberries, fed to me by my husband, so I decided I didn't want to eat the strawberries Al had gotten for me. Al got upset, and that's the sort of thing that could've turned into a silly fight, so before it got out of hand, I started laughing and I bent his finger back, and then he was laughing, and we moved right past the problem.

Sure it's important to get your point across, but it's more effective to chase it with something silly or stupid to lighten the situation. Unless it's the most serious matter you can think of, a silly argument or a tiff is never worth escalating for the sake of your pride.

I honestly don't even recall our biggest fights. Even at our worst, we are both looking for ways to stop the fight rather than add fuel to the fire. Some couples thrive on the drama of arguing. They love the passion and they love the makeup sex. I am not that person.

Screaming is no good in a relationship. When somebody screams all the time, the scream becomes less effective. Albert never raises his voice. I've only seen him lose it a couple of times, always at The Brownstone, and when that happens, you better run. But if he screamed like that all the time, nobody would listen. The secret to our arguing is that our goal as a couple has always been to make the other person laugh. Al has always said that my tears are his Kryptonite. He cannot stand to see me unhappy. If I cry, he literally cannot function. He will call me a million times until he thinks I'm

OK. This is why when we're arguing we don't ever get to the point of no return.

Al lost his father suddenly and tragically when he was so young. He learned very early in life that you never know if you'll see a person again. I know in my heart this is why he never wants to end any of our communication in a negative way. At the end of a disagreement, he'll always tell me he loves me and ask for a kiss. The big picture is always bigger than what we're dealing with.

I have a nervous laugh, so when I'm nervous about telling him something, I start laughing. Then he starts laughing, and whatever I have to tell him becomes a lot less serious. And this is how I've mastered the art of arguing so that my husband still loves me when we're done disagreeing.

My kids will all grow up and leave me one day to start families of their own, and nothing would make me happier.

As much as I have not loved the long hours that Albert worked, I have benefited from it, as it has permitted me to devote every night to my kids. Albert never felt the brunt of my dedication to the kids because he was never home. If he'd been home at five or six o'clock every night would I have been able to be the type of mother that I am? No way in hell. I compensated for the fact that he wasn't around too much by becoming a better mother. I could've instead surrounded myself with girlfriends and gone out to dinners with them when Al was working late, but that's not what makes me tick. There's nothing I'd rather be doing than hanging out with my kids.

I made sure I shared everything that the kids did with Albert; I kept them very connected. Even though his work caused him to miss important milestones in the kids' lives, I made sure I shared everything with him and kept them very connected. Even to this day we share everything, and that strong connection is the glue that holds our marriage together.

I know that Lauren and I will keep this kind of bond until I die. It's easier for mothers and daughters to be connected like that. But somewhere out there are two women who will come into my sons' lives and take them away from me. And that's fine. That's how it should be.

I'm absolutely ready to lose them to those women, if they're happy. You raise your kids to be happy, whole individuals, and all you want is for them to be content. When I married Albert, I became the most important woman in his life forever, until he dies. That's how it should be. I became his wife, and then the mother of his children.

I don't think it's going to be too tough when my boys get married. I will be the best mother-in-law on the planet. If you make my child smile, I will love you forever. I don't care if you're purple and paint yourself in green latex and do backflips through my house while you're yodeling. I don't care if you cook, I don't care if you clean, just make my child happy.

I've been with Albert for over thirty years now, and when that man walks in the door, my heart could explode. If he walked in right this second, I'd stop writing this book to hang out with him. To hell with you. That's the way I am. People tell us all the time that we beam when we see each other. That's my wish for my children, nothing more. To have the same bond with their spouse as their father and I have. When that person walks in the door I want my child to beam after thirty years.

I would like to be a mother-in-law that is around a lot. All three of the kids, in any relationship that they've had, I've become a friend to their partners. And I'm honestly looking forward to each of them marrying and moving on. It's the next phase in the life of this family, and I can't wait to be a part of it.

Ask Caroline

Hi Caroline: How do you balance making sure aging parents make good decisions and respecting their independence?

This is a tough one. We always think of our parents as superheroes and it's a sad moment when you realize that this isn't the case at all.

First and foremost, you need to define the issues at hand and see what kind of threat it represents. As an example; do they show signs of dementia and therefore should not be driving or going out alone? That's something that needs to be addressed immediately and you can go to your family doctor for help with that.

Financial decisions can come into play as well. Just have a conversation with your parents and try to understand their mind-set when making certain decisions. Also ask yourself if you are concerned more for yourself or for them: are you worried about your inheritance being squandered, or are you really concerned for them? So what if they want to go on a cruise around the world, or if they aren't selling their house so they can—let them, they earned the money, they can spend it too. If they are not making financial decisions that will significantly affect their quality of life, just step back and keep a cautious eye.

Talk to your parents about what's going on and show them the respect they deserve. If you need to bring others in to help, such as doctors and accountants, do so with tact. Don't give them ultimatums or make decisions for them. Instead, involve them and let them know they still have control over their lives but you are there simply to dot all the I's and cross all the T's.

I hate it when my kids break up with someone.

I always become friends with the people my children have in their lives. And when they break up with them, I always cry. I tell my boys I'm getting tired of falling in love with these girls, they break up with them, and it's like I break up with them! I am sick of it.

I'm going through the most complicated version of this right now. Albie's dating this girl, Lindsay, and I love her. I'm not sure if they're going to make it, but I know that I care for her deeply and I want to be there for her, regardless of what is going on between her and Albie.

Viewers of the show will know Lindsay, she was a big part of season four. She moved into that madhouse apartment in Hoboken with Albie, Chris, and Greg, and I knew it was a mistake. She was basically dating a full house, with a TV show being filmed at the same time. For a young girl who'd led a sheltered life, it was too much to handle. So she decided to move out.

She made this decision to move while Albie was in California on

Ask Caroline

What's the deal with Greg? Is he single?

Greg is a great guy, but he's taken! He is seeing a nice young man from Baltimore who's studying to be a plastic surgeon.

a business trip. Lindsay and Lauren have become good friends, and Lauren was the one who told me that Lindsay had decided to move out—and she was moving the next day.

I was shocked, but I was more surprised by what I heard next: Lindsay planned to do the whole move by herself. She was going to hire a taxi for the day and just move herself into a fourth-floor walkup. I called her right away and said, "I'm not going to take no for an answer, I'll be at your place at eleven to help you move."

I took Lauren with me, and it ultimately took the three of us three days to move all her stuff, in the back of my truck. I developed bursitis in my shoulder from lugging all that crap up four flights of stairs. During the move, Albie told me to take his entire bedroom set and give it to Lindsay, and that he'd sleep on the couch when he got back from California.

When we were finished moving her into her new place, I looked around and noticed that all she had was lots and lots of clothes and lots of personal items, but absolutely none of the essentials that you need to set up house.

That night I went home and went through my basement, through all those boxes that we all accumulate over the years, and pulled out boxes of unopened cutlery, glasses, pots, plates, and other stuff she needed. I packed up my truck the next day and took it over to her.

Throughout the move, I kept thinking, if this were my child, I'd hope someone would take care of her like this. The first night she moved, she had nothing, and I invited her to sleep at my house. She didn't want to, but I insisted.

Later that night, Al could tell something wasn't right with me, and he asked what was bothering me. As I tried to answer I just burst into tears.

"This poor thing," I said. "She's going to be going to an empty apartment every night. She walks up forty-eight steps alone to an empty apartment. She doesn't have any family around her, she has nobody." Al just looked at me with those big eyes. Then he said, "Stop crying, tomorrow we'll go buy furniture for her apartment!"

As I said before, Al says that my tears are his Kryptonite. He can't bear to see me cry. He can't function when I'm sad. So the next day we went and furnished her entire apartment. I didn't tell her what I'd done, but I had to call her and tell her to take the following Tuesday off work. She asked why, and I told her because her furniture was coming.

I explained it was my way of saying thank you for making my son happy and that I hoped they could work things out but if not, that was OK too. She was helping Lauren in her store, and in the early days of Cafface we couldn't afford to pay her much, so the furniture was my way of saying thank you. It gave me peace of mind.

When she went home that day, she had a home.

I told Albie that Lindsay came into his life, and whether she stays with him or not, she also came into my life. And one day when he becomes a father, he'll understand why I did what I did for her.

PART V

BODY

I'm fifty-one, but in my head I'm seventeen.

Every day, I forget that I'm middle-aged. I still have the same spunk and drive that I had when I was seventeen. I still have the same excitement about trying new things—like signing on to do the show. Back then, I would have taken the bull by the horns and given it my all. Today nothing has changed. I still want to ride the wave and see where it takes me.

The only difference now is that when I look in the mirror, I see my mother staring back at me. I look down and see my mother's hands. And that's always a shock. "Where the hell did you come from?" I ask my reflection. That's when it hits me, I'm fifty-one.

In my mind, I'm seventeen, but physically my body is starting to feel fifty. I used to be able to run so fast; I loved to run. Now I can't. My eyesight is shot. I can't see a damned thing. When I helped Lindsay move into her fourth-floor walkup, I thought nothing of it—until I developed bursitis and needed heavy painkillers, getting cortisone shots in my shoulder!

Once I realized that my body was starting to get creaky, I decided that if I want to remain seventeen in my head and not be limited by my age, I needed to keep this body of mine as healthy as possible. My body needs to be as fit and active as my mind. I got busy.

Al built an amazing gym in the basement for the boys when they were teenagers. It's time for me to start using it. I even went and got a trainer who's going to come and make sure I do. I'm lifting weights and stretching and getting myself back into fighting shape. So far, so good, although it hurt like a bitch for the first month—but I just remind myself that it's going to take work if I want to keep thinking that I'm seventeen!

I've always eaten in moderation; I've always known when to stop. But hitting fifty has been a huge wake-up call. I don't metabolize as quickly as I used to.

I'm very conscious now of how I eat. I can't eat a dozen chocolate chip cookies at midnight anymore. I have to treat my body better than that. I've started eating fewer carbs, smaller portions, and more protein.

I'm not in denial. I'm not trying to freeze time. We all age, second by second by second. But I'm going to try to preserve myself as well as I can because I want to be around for a lot longer. Heart disease, high blood pressure, diabetes, all these things are now circling me, and I don't want anything to do with them.

I have a husband who's young at heart. I have three kids who keep me on my toes. And one day I hope to have grandchildren who will make me laugh. I'm going to do the best I can to be healthy enough so that my body can be almost as agile as my seventeen-year-old spirit. Let me tell you, I'm going to be the most kick-ass eighty-year-old you ever saw.

My secrets to healthy eating

1. Greek yogurt with blueberries and a shot of agave nectar is my breakfast. It used to be nothing. I'm not a breakfast person. This gets me started nicely, and the yogurt is great for the digestive system.
2. I used to love chips and Doritos, and now I snack on an apple with some cheese.
3. Dinner is now grilled chicken and sautéed vegetables with olive oil. I love vegetables, even steamed.
4. If I want lasagna or something carby, I'll just control my portion. If I want a cheeseburger, I'll buy one, but I'll only eat a quarter of it.
5. The only dessert I will eat anymore is fresh fruit. Luckily, I love fresh fruit and was never much of a dessert person.

My workout routine

1. Start with a minimum of forty-five minutes on the treadmill, five days a week. Set the speed to 4.0 and the incline as high as you can manage it.
2. Three sets of fifteen triceps dips. I hold a medicine ball above my head and slowly lower it behind my head.
3. Three sets of twelve squats while holding a kettle-bell between your legs.
4. Sit-ups are important for core strength, and I love them. I have a belly cruncher. I can go and do sets of fifty until I get up to a thousand. Some days are better than others. On some days, I only do two hundred.
5. Leg extensions, around a hundred per day.
6. Stationary bike—it's just not for me. I find the routine that I like and stick with it.

Always try to look your best; there's no reason to scare yourself every time you pass the mirror.

Looking your best is easy. I know, you're probably thinking "easy for you, if you have a team of stylists getting you ready for a Bravo taping." But it really doesn't take a lot of time, and it doesn't take a lot of props to look good. I'm not talking about six-inch heels and a full face of makeup. If that's your thing, fine. But if you've watched me on the show, you'll know I'm OK with keeping my beauty routine, more . . . natural. When I say look your best, I mean put in some effort. As women juggling it all, it's easy to give up in the beauty department. But shampoo your hair, tidy up your nails. Make sure your clothes are clean and that they fit nicely! Nobody wants to see you looking like a hot mess with dirty, unkempt hair, chewed nails, and spaghetti sauce down your shirt. You can wear jeans, a T-shirt, and flat shoes and still look like a million bucks. In fact, that's my go-to look.

Don't get me wrong—I love to get dressed up. I love silly clothes. I love skinny jeans. But at fifty-one, I will only wear those skinny jeans with a blouse and ballet flats, not with Louboutins and a low-cut top. That's not age appropriate for me. I don't want to dress like my daughter, I want to dress like me.

It doesn't matter what shape you are, you need to first be aware of your age, and your stature. If you're a mom and a wife, you need to dress in a way that doesn't shame your family. With my body, it's too easy for me to look like Jessica Rabbit. I'm short and I'm a bundle of curves. The last thing my kids need to see is me leaving nothing to the imagination. It's just creepy when a mom tries to be too sexual in front of her kids. I've never been into fads or current fashion. I think the key is to know your body and what clothing suits your body best.

BEHIND THE SCENES

People criticized me for not dressing up for my brother Jamie's wedding rehearsal dinner. Of course there's a story there. Our flights kept getting canceled on our way to Chicago, and by the time we landed, we were super late. Production instructed us to go directly to the rehearsal dinner, and we were not allowed to go to our hotel and change. It had been a long day, and there I was, dressed in my travel sweats without a scrap of makeup on my face. At the same time, Chris had a stomach flu. People wrote the cruelest things about that one—that I didn't care about my appearance, and that I really need to cut the apron strings with Chris. My son was sick, and getting sicker. We had to keep stopping the bus so he could throw up. And I'm getting criticized for it? Sometimes I wish that we could get more of the backstory onto the show, but since we can't, I just put on a brave face and let the haters hate.

I don't have a complicated beauty regime or secrets to share either. I have beautiful skin because my mother has beautiful skin.

You don't have to use expensive creams—but the bottom line is, your face needs moisturizer. It doesn't know the difference between the five-buck baby lotion from the drugstore and the most expensive luxurious cream from the department store. I used to put baby oil or Vaseline on my face at night and wake up with the smoothest, softest face. I also never ever go out in the sun anymore. When I was younger I loved tanning, but I'm too fair-skinned, and I don't want to end up looking like a prune just to try to get bronzed. These days I buy the highest SPF I can find; I usually wear the one they make for children. I have to be so careful. Ten minutes in the sun, and I'm in trouble.

My beauty routine each day, including my shower, is under a half hour. I wear little or no makeup. Sometimes I even forget to put makeup on for the red carpet. I get all the way to an event and realize I forgot. I just shrug and say, *screw it*, I'm not here because these people love me for my long fake eyelashes. I'd like to think they like me for what I stand for.

But even without the makeup, I always make sure I look presentable. If you think you've become a hot mess, turn it around. Be the best you there is. You've got three kids and no time? I was there. If you have to shampoo your hair at 2:00 AM, so be it. I used to put all three kids on the bathroom floor while I showered. I'd give them games to play and I'd pop my head out of the shower every two minutes and check on them. There's no reason for sloppiness. You should never look like you just got dragged through mud. Take a little care with yourself, take a little pride in yourself, and you'll be amazed at how much better everything else feels . . .

A clean-shaven . . . face?

My one beauty secret is that I shave my face every day. I'm not a hairy person, I've never had peach fuzz on my face. It's a matter of exfoliation, it takes off the top layer of dead skin, and I swear by it.

People always laugh at me when I talk about it, and that's fine. They can. About fifteen years ago, my sister went for a facial, and the beautician she went to was a gorgeous Swedish woman of about seventy. She was amazed by how beautiful she was and asked how she managed to keep looking so young and vibrant. She was so shocked

My favorite beauty products

1. Darphin is a phenomenal skin care line.
2. Dr. Perricone's Skin and Total Body Supplements are great for my skin—they're a collection of vitamins that you take daily.
3. Kiehl's lip balm is my secret weapon.
4. Giorgio Armani and Makeup Forever foundations are my absolute favorites.
5. Laura Mercier tinted moisturizer and foundation match my skin perfectly.
6. L'Oréal mascara is the best, and it's cheap at the drugstore!

when the woman told her that she shaved her face every day, and that was how she kept her skin looking so great.

I shave from just under my eyes all the way down my face and down my neck. It was never a matter of hair. I can go three weeks without shaving my legs. I don't know if this would work for someone who has a bit more fuzz on their face, but I don't get any bristles or any rough patches. Quite the opposite—I just get smooth, glowing skin. I don't even use shaving cream—I just do it in the shower every day with whatever soap I'm using. See? This is what I'm talking about—you just take a few minutes extra each day and put yourself together.

People think my job is glamorous—but I think photo shoots are hell!

Let's get one thing straight: I'm not photogenic at all. I know this, and I'm OK with it. And yet here I am, working in a medium in which photo shoots are a fact of life.

I hate seeing myself in pictures in magazines. I'm probably the only Housewife who never looks at the proofs when we do photo shoots. As soon as we are done, everyone runs over to the computer

Lauren Manzo's five-minute face

Make sure your skin is always clean and healthy, that will give you a head start to always look great! Exfoliate, moisturize, and apply masks regularly. Try to avoid letting your skin dry out. If you keep it nice and moisturized, it will help with makeup application and prevent aging.

(continued)

1. Take a corrector concealer pen in a peachy color and pat it under your eyes to correct dark circles.

2. Take an olive concealer and put that on any blemish.

3. Next, put a tinted moisturizer over your whole face. It's key to have your exact shade, so go to a salon like Cafface and have them pick your shade for you. Always go a little lighter than your skin tone, and make sure it blends.

4. Next, it's time for either a light pressed powder or a bronzer, depending on your skin tone and your goal. Less is always more when it comes to powder. I like a little bronzer right on my cheeks and a bit under my chin, just to contour the face. Again, blending is key.

5. Get a light peachy blush, and just lightly apply to the apple of your cheeks. When you smile, it's the curved, rounded part of each cheek.

6. Finally, apply a light mascara. Start at the very root of your lash and wiggle the brush at the base of the eyelash, then brush it out. Don't worry about eye shadow—this is your five-minute face. You're going for a nearly nude, clean look. If you want to do a light eyeliner, use a nice color like a green or purple, but just apply it lightly on the outer edges of your eyes.

7. For everyday, a nice light lip is fine. If you have naturally pink lips, just use balm. Otherwise, use a lightly tinted balm, or a good gloss. You're going for a fresh look, so don't overdo it.

to see what the pictures have turned out like. Not me. I thank the photographer and I walk away.

What's the point? I'm probably not going to like what I see, and there's nothing I can do about it. They can't reshoot the whole day.

I've never been comfortable posing in front of a camera, but I know it's part of my job, so I suck it up. To me, it doesn't feel natural to be smiling just because you're being told to. When I'm in front of a photographer, and he just keeps saying "SMILE!" over and over, smiling is the last thing I feel like doing. It's crazy when you're on the red carpet and you see people who know exactly how to position themselves for the hundreds of cameras. They stand perfectly still and they move their face from left to right, slowly. They probably stop eight times, and each time they give the perfect angle to the photographers. I can't even conceive of trying to do this. Look at my red carpet photos! I'm a mess of stupid expressions, double chins, and blurry hands.

BEHIND THE SCENES

Lauren has done my makeup for the last three reunion shows. She does Jacqueline's too. She also does our makeup for all the interview sessions that we film during the season. I love it—she helps me relax in between takes and keeps my sanity intact. She also gets paid for these makeup jobs, so it's a great booking for her, professionally. When it comes to the regular day-to-day shooting, I do my own makeup. I'm not great, but I'm getting better at it. Next season, I think I'll just pop into Cafface in the mornings before I film my scenes.

I see the same photographers at every event. I recognize their faces and I even know some of their names. So when I see them,

Caroline's tips for posing for photos

Even though I hate photo shoots, I've learned a few simple tips that will help you look like a star in front of the camera.

1. Always cross your ankles, with one foot slightly back behind the other. This gives your legs a more slender line.
2. Put your weight on one leg, and gently bend the other one.
3. Turn your hips on a slight angle toward the camera. That will make them look a lot less wide.
4. Raise your chin and try to keep your face toward the lens of the camera.
5. Learn the planes of your face. We all have an "angle" that works for us. Spend some time practicing in the mirror!
6. Don't stare down the camera. Try to make eye contact with the photographer, if you can, or just focus on his forehead if not.
7. Be natural. Smile like you would if someone told you a joke.
8. Put one hand on your hip, and let the other hand rest on your thigh. Avoid letting your free hand hang awkwardly.

I'm waving hi or asking them if they're doing OK; I'm not thinking about sticking my chest out and positioning my legs so I look thinner than I am. I don't care if I make it onto the worst dressed lists either. I've had good outfits, bad outfits, and wardrobe malfunctions. I've posed in sparkly dresses in New York's best photo studios. What gets me through the awkwardness of these shoots is the knowledge that one day, all of this will just be something to amuse my grandchildren.

What I really love are candid photos. If you look around my house, you'll notice that 90 percent of the photos I've put in frames are candid. These photos show real moments, they capture real smiles. That's the way I like to be photographed: when I am not expecting it, and when I'm focused on something else that makes me happy. Some of the best photos of me are ones that Albert has taken without my knowledge, of me laughing at a joke or smiling at someone. There are plenty of pictures of me with no makeup on, playing with my kids or hanging out with my husband, and I love them. It doesn't matter if you look good in photos, it matters if you like the memory they capture for you. I'm constantly taking photos with my phone of my kids, my nephews and nieces. I never ask them to pose or fake it, I just try to capture moments that I want to remember.

Photos, for me, are heirlooms. They're memories. And that's why it's important to keep them honest and pure. Next time someone tells you to smile when you don't feel like it, just let your face do whatever it wants. Show them how you feel, and the rest will fall into place.

This face is mine and I'm not going to change it!

There are so many times I look in the mirror with my hands placed on either side of my forehead, tightly pulling my skin back and up. I fleetingly think, "Ooh, I should do this or that, I could nip this and tuck that." And then I snap out of it, take a step back, really look at my face with all of its flaws and realize: this is me. I've been living with my face my whole life. It's not the best face, nor is it the most beautiful, but it's the one I was born with. It's my face and it's what I was given and it's what I'm going to wear. I'll wear it the best way I know how, and I'll do it with confidence.

As much as I like to look my best, I'm not that concerned with beauty at all. I have decided that I'm going to be happy with whatever time does to my face, and I'll work with what I've got naturally.

Think about people that you've known in your life who could be considered plain. As you've gotten to know them and seen their qualities, they've become beautiful to you. Personality makes a person shine, it really does. A great sense of humor can add sparkle to a person's eyes. A kind heart can brighten someone's smile. Personality can do a lot more to make you beautiful than a face-lift!

In my opinion, plastic surgery doesn't turn back the clock as much as it turns you into someone else. I see a lot of women who've

By the bottle

My natural hair color is brown. Plain, mousy brown. These days it's also going gray really quickly. I first went red when I was very young. One day I went to the salon and the woman asked if I wanted to go red. I said sure, and that was that. I didn't think about it, but I liked it and I've stuck with it. I don't really care too much about my hair, I figure that the hairstylist knows more about hair than I do, so I let them do whatever they think is best. I don't' stress about it, and if I hate what they do, I know it'll grow out pretty quickly. The red was never premeditated, but I love it. It's so much brighter than my mousy brown. These days, they do low lights and highlights and all this other stuff, and it looks great. I'll stay a redhead for the rest of my life!

had face-lifts in an attempt to look younger. But they don't look younger. In fact, all of their faces end up looking the same, especially if they went to the same plastic surgeon! They're not fooling anyone. When I come across these ladies, all I see is an older woman who's had a face-lift. No matter how hard she tries to cheat Father Time, she'll never win.

I'm happy for my face to look fifty-one. Accepting the changes that aging will bring will make me beautiful as I get older. I always meet women who swear by their surgeon. They tell me that if I just get "a little thing" done here and there, "nobody will know" that I've been under the knife. Yes, somebody will know: me. I just can't do it.

I could think of nothing worse than getting a face-lift and no longer looking like the mother my kids have known their whole lives. I wouldn't look like the girl Al married, and that would break his heart. I know I'm going to look just like my mother when I get old, and that's perfectly okay.

But like I said, if you think that a face-lift will make you happy, go right ahead. For me, I want my grandkids to look at my own face, not a science project.

Don't touch my face, but tuck my tummy away.

I know a lot of people who had substantial plastic surgery, and I'm actually OK with it if that's what they want. I don't have anything against plastic surgery or people who choose to get it. I just would never want to do anything that would alter my face, my expressions, my personal identity.

But in the spirit of full disclosure, I had a tummy tuck when I was forty. I'd had three kids, and I had this tiny little pouch of skin that sagged over the front of my pants. I used to call it the baby's ass.

That's just what it looked like. I went to the surgeon, and he told me that no amount of diet or exercise could ever make it go away. The elasticity was gone.

At that time, I had to buy my pants two sizes bigger to accommodate this pouch, and it was just no fun anymore. I wanted to buy pants that fit. So I said screw it and went in for the tummy tuck. They removed two pounds of excess skin around my waist, and I was able to buy pants in my size. I'm not ashamed to talk about it.

On the flip side, I have always refused to get my breasts reduced. My chest is so big, and that comes with a lot of inconveniences—the backaches—and there's the fact that I'm very short, so I always look top-heavy. But for some reason, I just can't bring myself to do it.

I tell myself my tummy tuck was a practical decision. A breast reduction would be more frivolous. I can always buy a size twelve top and have it altered down to a six so that it fits my chest and waist. I could never get pants altered in a way that fit nicely when I had my tummy pouch.

I'll never say never, but I'm pretty positive that I'm done with plastic surgery for the rest of my life.

My sons will never see me in a bikini!

We are living in a MILF world. Women in their forties and fifties are starting to think it's OK to dress like twenty-year-old club kids. It drives me crazy. As much as I love my body, I think it would make my sons uncomfortable to see me in a bikini, and I will never ever wear one in front of them!

I am not a fan of women who think it's cool to wear bikinis around their kid's friends. There's nothing good about being a MILF. Grow up. If you have to be something, be a WILF, be a wife that somebody wants to, you know. But don't do it around your own

Lauren's weight struggle— in her own words

I've always been a big kid. When I was younger, I was heavy, and I remember my grandma asking me how old I was. I remember thinking that she knew exactly how old I was, but she thought I was big for my age. I've been aware of my weight my entire life.

My mom would always get certain outfits for me and she'd buy me things like cargo shorts instead of the tiny shorts my skinny friends were wearing, or I'd have to wear boardshorts instead of a bikini. I could never have the cool clothes I wanted because of my size. I wore jerseys and overalls because I hated how I looked.

My mom knew I was miserable and she always tried to help me lose weight by making me eat healthful food and talking to me about exercise, but I hated her for it. I didn't want to change my habits. And it felt like everyone was talking about my weight when I wasn't in the room.

When I was a teenager, my dad got me a personal trainer, and for a while that was great, but that was also the start of my yo-yo dieting. I'd lose and gain, over and over, and my mom was always the one to give me a look when I was eating something bad. Now, in hindsight, I know she was trying to help me because she could see how depressed I was over my size.

I look at Vito and I, and how we're both genetically predisposed to being overweight. I know that if we have kids, they're going to be freakin' huge. And I'm

(continued)

going to have to be even tougher on my kids than my mom was on me. I don't want my own kids to have the same struggles that I had and that Vito still has.

This year, I got my lap band surgery, and it has changed my life. I have been forced to change all my eating habits, and I've lost a lot of weight. It bothers me that people think my family forced me to do this. People say horrible things, like my family accepts me now that I'm thinner. That's so not the case.

My family's concern was always my happiness. That's why it was annoying when people said that my family was being mean to me about my weight. My mom has fat days, and she'll say she's eight pounds of sausage in a five-pound bag, and it's nuts that people gave her grief for saying that about me on the TV show. I *was* eight pounds of sausage in a five-pound bag. I was 185 pounds. I needed to make a change. That's when I decided to get my lap band surgery.

I've always used humor to deal with my weight, and so has my family. I nicknamed my tummy Timothy. Right now he's called Tim because I've lost a lot of weight. If I lose all my weight, I'll call him T. I've been trying to break up with him my whole life. Every now and then he goes on vacation, but he comes back.

Ultimately, I know that humor and love and support from my family have been the things that got me through my issues with weight. I don't care if people don't understand where I'm coming from or want to make a dumb comment about my weight or family, because I know the truth about my family: That their motivation was my happiness, and it still is, no matter what I weigh.

kids. Save the cougar act for your next girls' trip to Vegas. If I go away with my husband, I'm going to wear a bikini. Let me tell you, at fifty-one, I'm proud that I can still wear a bikini and look good. But that's for him. It's private, between us.

Look at Melissa Gorga. She's gorgeous, she has a killer body. But I bet, as her boys get older, she's going to get a little more modest in how she dresses. It's something that just happens. If you think your son's friends are checking you out, cover up fast.

It's not hard to impress a hormonal teenage boy by parading in front of him in a bikini, but imagine the teasing your kids are going to get at school if they have the hot mom. Being a good parent is much more important than using your kids' friends for validation!

BEHIND THE SCENES

We all dress ourselves on the show! People always tell me how great it must be to be given all these clothes to wear on TV. We are never given a wardrobe; everything you see on TV is something that I went out and bought for myself. I don't get sent free clothes from designers—I wish!—I just make do with what I have in the closet. Even for reunion shows, we dress ourselves, but at those times, Bravo will suggest what color we can dress in. Then they send a stylist to our house to photograph us in what we want to wear, and a couple of other options that they choose from our wardrobe. After Bravo looks at the photos, we find out what we are permitted to wear. But it's still our own clothing!

There are so many wonderful options when it comes to sexy beachwear. You don't have to wear a thong and a string bra-top to the beach to make a splash. There are all kinds of wraps and sheer

Ask Caroline

Caroline: As I age, my metabolism is slowing down more each year. How do you fight this and keep your figure?

Ughhh, tell me about it! This is a huge struggle for me and I'm sure many other men and women out there too!

As we age, our metabolism slows down and we start to lose muscle mass. We have to almost reinvent ourselves and our way of life to accommodate the changes in our body.

Because we have less muscle mass, we burn fewer calories. Therefore our calorie intake should change; our body can sustain itself on fewer calories. It's not the same as when we were younger. Everyone is built differently so I suggest you see a professional nutritionist or your doctor for guidance.

Another thing we need to do is exercise more! Try to get yourself in the gym or walking or jogging at least three times a week—every day if you can!

You'll feel better, I promise!

Get plenty of sleep; studies show that lack of sleep can contribute to weight gain (not to mention it makes you grumpy!).

Drink plenty of water; I carry a water bottle around with me constantly.

Good luck, and welcome to the club.

tops that hint at your body and make you look incredible, while still keeping things modest.

When I go to the beach or a pool with my boys, I will always err on the side of caution. I'll wear a one-piece, with a wrap around my waist, or a full-length sheer sundress over my bathing suit. I still feel like I look great, and I don't have to worry about anyone feeling uncomfortable—including myself!

So next Memorial Day, don't sweat about losing those ten pounds of winter weight. Spend your time picking the most gorgeous one-piece and sundress you can find, and make your kids proud. Realize that sexy comes in many forms, and you'll have a much more relaxed summer!

PART VI

LIFE

I'm a badass with a heart; I cry at Kodak commercials.

It's very likely that you may have judged me wrong. Most people I meet because of the TV show are surprised that I'm friendly, open-minded and not as matriarchal as I am on the show. And now that you're getting to know me, I figure it's time we can share a secret. I'm a softie.

Don't get me wrong—I am very strong. I am very determined. I have my feet solidly planted on the ground, but I'm also sweet and I can be vulnerable.

When I look at myself, I still see the shy child I was. At school, I never thought anyone wanted to be my friend. I would sit alone in the lunchroom and not talk to another soul. I never went to dances; I didn't socialize with my school companions very much at all. Imagine my surprise when, after I left school, I found out that all the football players had wanted to date me, but they thought I was aloof and they didn't know how to approach me.

BEHIND THE SCENES

I can't stop mothering my crew. My mothering instincts just kick in whenever I see something wrong with one of them. Last winter, one of my producers was so sick with the flu, coughing and blowing her nose constantly. Right in the middle of a scene, I couldn't take it anymore, so I went to my medicine chest—with the whole crew following me and filming—and I got some Theraflu out, pointed at her, and told her to take it right there on the spot. She was shaking her head no, but I insisted. Some people say they get so used to the cameras that they forget they are there, but I'm not wired that way. My crew are guests in my home, so I take care of them.

The source of my shyness came from a feeling of being "different." My family moved from New York to New Jersey in high school, and I just didn't fit in. Being one of eleven kids was a great education; it taught me how to negotiate. It taught me how to do without; it taught me loyalty. But it was a double-edged sword, because my family, my sisters and brothers, were my best friends back then. I had little incentive to come out of my shell at school and socialize with others.

I'm most content just sitting and watching people. I can sit and watch people for hours; I wonder what their stories are. I study body language. And I'm very good at reading people. I'm very intuitive. For whatever reason, I don't know if I'm half a witch or what, but I have a very good sense of what people are feeling.

BEHIND THE SCENES

One of the most frustrating things about doing the show is that we never know where the season is going, but the producers do. Those guys hear what all of us are saying, so they know everyone's secrets. They know which feuds are brewing and when they are likely to explode. No matter how hard you beg them to let you in on what's happening, they will never tell you. We never ever have a script to follow, but we are told to turn up at certain events or places. What happens at these meetings are our real reactions because we honestly don't know what we're in for. But it's incredibly hard when you are walking into an event, and you don't know if it's going to be fun, or an ambush.

More often than not you will never know what's going on in my mind. I'm happiest being quiet and letting you do the talking.

That's why it's so weird that I have the opposite reputation on

TV. I believe fighting, yelling, and controversy get you nowhere. But I'm surrounded by it on the show. What am I supposed to do? Back down? I never back down. And if I'm wrong, I will apologize. I owed a huge apology to Kathy and Melissa at the end of season three. I had been fed misinformation about them, and rather than checking with them, I just assumed that they were not my friends. I treated them poorly as a result. I regret what I said to them and how it blew out of proportion. I have since apologized, but I know I was wrong to do what I did, and that makes me feel awful about it to this day.

Reflecting on the *Real Housewives* seasons I feel I've been fair on the show. I've called people on their bullshit, but for the most part, I've actually sat on the sidelines for a lot of the big drama. I haven't been manipulative or evil in any way.

What makes me cry

1. When old people are abused or are having a hard life. It really breaks my heart. If I see an old bag lady in the winter, I lose it.

2. Anytime my kids are upset, my tears aren't far behind.

3. Whenever I see a report of child abuse. I cry, then I want to go hunt down the people who did it.

4. Any natural disaster; I think of the people trapped and worried and concerned for their families. I can't imagine how awful it would be to go through something like that.

5. Any child with a life-threatening disease. I was blessed with three healthy children, and when I hear of someone finding out their child has a serious illness, it devastates me.

I truly hate to hurt people. Seeing people suffer makes me cry. I'll be driving in Manhattan with my husband, and I'll see a homeless woman. Immediately I imagine her life, and how hard it is, and I'll start to cry. I cry easily at the upsetting things in the world.

Some may say I'm overly sensitive, but my sensitivity defines me, and has made me into a nurturing and caring mother, wife, and friend.

So if you meet me hoping to see some fireworks, you're likely to be disappointed. I'm actually a very quiet person. Well, I'm as quiet as a mouse until someone backs me up against a wall and takes a swing at me or my family. In that case, get out of my way. Run as fast as you can.

Book smarts are great, but without street smarts and personality, you got nothing.

I've been surrounded by smart people my whole life, some of them have degrees from the best schools in the world, some of them never finished high school. And as much as I respect someone pursuing an education, that degree ain't worth the paper it's printed on if you don't have street smarts to go with it.

Book smarts will get you through the door, but your personality will keep you in the room. No matter how qualified you are, you have to be able to talk and be truly engaging to get anywhere in life. If you don't have that, who cares what a piece of paper says?

I did not go to college. My parents had to care and pay for eleven children, and I didn't want to burden them with the cost of sending me to school. I dreamed of becoming a child psychologist or an attorney, that's what I really wanted to be. But I knew that my dad needed me at his work. I graduated high school, and the next day I started work in his office. I didn't go to the yearbook signing party;

I didn't go to my prom. And to this day, I consider going to work for my dad to be one of the smartest decisions I've ever made.

I did his books, ran his office, handled his creditors, and learned to think fast. That job made me who I am today. My time with my dad, being by his side, watching him at work, was invaluable. My dad never even finished high school, but he is literally a genius. We would start each workday with a stop at the church to say a prayer. My dad was a hard worker, but he didn't forget the important things in life, and he didn't take anything for granted.

One of the most valuable experiences I had in my dad's office, as awful as it was at the time, was being there as his business fell apart. His company dealt in plastics, and suddenly there was a shortage of the plastic pellets he needed for his business. It crippled my father's company. I remember working the phones and having to bullshit my way through all these phone calls. I was eighteen, juggling customers and creditors, and helping my dad keep his head above water.

I saw him fail, I saw him fall, and I saw him pick himself up again because he had to, for his family. It made me so proud of my father. I worked for him until right before I got married at twenty-two. I saw the good, the bad, and the ugly, and I learned what to do in business, and what not to do. That was the best education I could ever have gotten.

My father was a pit bull in business. When things got ugly, he was a madman. He taught me the value of managing a group and understanding its dynamics. There's always one leader in a group, and at least one bad apple. Learning to tell the difference has always helped me in business and in life.

I'm probably gonna get a lot of shit for this, but I don't care. I'm going to say this: it is my feeling that if you don't go to college for a very specific thing, like to become a doctor, a lawyer, a scientist, an architect, something very specific, don't go. If you're going to college just to have the college experience, don't waste your friggin' money.

I'd estimate that 90 percent of the people I know who've graduated from a university are not doing what they went to college for. Life gets in the way of many career plans, so if you aren't gonna be a doctor, save your money. Get out there, pound the pavement, identify what you want to do with your life, and go after it with everything you can. Be a warrior.

If you don't have a degree and you want a job that requires one, go in there and stand up for yourself. Tell them that you may not have a degree but you're a badass and you're good at what you do. Then tell them that if they give you the job, they can pay you half the salary for two months, and you'll show them. Remind them that someday in their past someone took a chance on them. Be honest, have balls, show initiative.

A degree is only as good as what you intend to use it for. Albie's business degree from Fordham is hanging on the wall in my office, and it makes me proud, but I'm just as proud of my other kids, who didn't go to college. Lauren went to a trade school and learned to be a cosmetologist. And Christopher went to the school of life. I had all three possible educational experiences with my kids—college, no college, and trade school. And they're all equally successful.

Albie's using his degree in business with his brother, but Christopher is the bait and hook. He gets the meeting, he uses his street smarts to keep potential clients interested, and then Albie comes in with his business knowledge to close the deal. Together they're dynamic, they're a great team. Christopher is the guy you want to go out on the golf course with; he's the guy you want sitting at the bar with you. It's his street smarts that save the day, every time. Christopher learned something in the real world that you just can't learn in college: how to read people and how to keep them engaged and earn their trust. It's always having these qualities, as well as a college degree, that make a business a success.

I laugh a lot. At myself. And so should you. Humor will get you through the hard times.

The thing that bugs me most about *Real Housewives* is that they always make me look so damn serious. The fact is, that couldn't be further from the truth: I'm probably the most easygoing person on that show.

I love to laugh. Most of the day, there's a smile on my face. I know that doesn't make for great reality TV, but it's me. I've gotten through every tough time in my life by laughing, and not always at the right things.

In 1983 my husband lost his father, and afterward, my mother-in-law's house was overrun by people. It was a crazy, dark, intense time. Everyone was dealing with the shock of his loss, and the sadness of his absence. He was a popular man, and the visitors kept flooding in to pay their respects. When you thought that the house couldn't hold another person, there'd be twenty more people at the door.

After a full day of visitors the family just wanted to be alone, and tensions were starting to rise. I went into the kitchen with Al's aunt Joan to make the fifty thousandth pot of coffee for the newest batch of visitors. She and I looked at each other funny, and I quipped "Should we make some coffee?" which was what we'd been doing all day. Suddenly, we both burst out laughing. We cracked up so hard that we ended up on the floor, laughing at God knows what—who knows!

I'll always remember she sent me a letter afterward, telling me that our laughing fit got her through one of the toughest days of her life.

BEHIND THE SCENES

My kids and I always try to make the camera guys crack up. It's the worst thing they can do, because if they make a noise, the shot is ruined and they'll get their ass kicked. So, of course, it's a goal of ours to tell a sudden shocking joke or do a visual stunt that makes our camera guy laugh out loud. I honestly hope that one day they'll do a bloopers reel of all this hilarious stuff that didn't make it on air, so that you guys can see how much fun we had making the show. It's hysterical.

Laughing gives such a release. Sometimes a good laugh can derail a good cry. Though I do get a little embarrassed when a laughing fit comes on during a less-than-appropriate time. Without fail, I will erupt into giggles at a viewing before a funeral if the deceased is wearing glasses. I can't explain it. I don't mean to be disrespectful. I mean it's the most ridiculous thing. Put the glasses in their hands, or in the pocket of their jacket. Those glasses certainly are not going to help them see any better now. Al is getting pretty good at explaining that one—people stare at him, as if I'm deranged for laughing. He just nods understandingly and says "it's the glasses." The harder I try to mask the laughter, the worse it gets. But, hey, it beats the heck out of crying!

I was dreadful when it came to disciplining the kids when they were little. They'd make a silly mistake, and you'd have to let them have it. But they would always look so cute and they'd say the cutest things that I could never keep a straight face. I would leave the room and just crumble into fits of laughter while Al kept up the bad-cop routine.

Lauren especially would get me going. Al's favorite band is Queen, so we were always listening to their music at home. Little Lauren loved the music too, so much that she made a sign, using the

lyrics from one of their songs, and hung it on her bedroom door—
AND NOW YOU CAN KISS MY ASS GOOD-BYE. She was so proud of herself.
When I saw it I laughed so hard I was crying, but we had to try to
show her why it was wrong. Thankfully Al can keep a straighter face
than I!

Much worse was the time when she was ten, and the boys decided
to trick her by telling her that the word *jerk off* was a term of endearment! On that day we had family visiting. Al's mother came up to
Lauren to greet her. "Hi, Lala, how are you?" she said. You can imagine my mother-in-law's horror when her darling granddaughter
turned to her and said, smiling sweetly, "Hi, jerk off!" I couldn't
believe what I was hearing, but then I saw Albie and Christopher bust
up laughing, and I knew they'd set her up. I saw the humor in it, and
whenever I remember that moment, it still brings a smile to my face.

I try to keep my humor respectful. Nobody likes being laughed
at. I used to hate it, but I've been forced by the show to come to
terms with it. You need to develop a thick skin and learn how to
laugh it off once you decide to make your life public. Everyone on
the Web has an opinion, and it was tough at first. It still can be.

In season four, we featured Lauren's weight struggle on the show,
and I've always been so supportive of her. I was shocked when the
public reacted so poorly. They insisted that I was a bad parent for
humiliating my child in public. Lauren's decision to share her weight
battle was made by Lauren. Trust me—if she hadn't been comfortable with it being on TV, you wouldn't have seen a single mention of
it on the show. It's hard to laugh off the rude comments when they
are about your mothering.

As with any joke, how funny it is depends on who's pulling the
trigger. It's a fine line, and from time to time, my feelings can still
get hurt. If someone lashes out at my family, it still stings. But I'm
getting better at letting the personal insults roll off my back.

Laughter has helped with everything from grief to loss to fame.
Whether life is headed up or down, we have a choice between laughter and tears, and if I can help it, I'll choose laughter every time.

Ask Caroline

Caroline, I'm at my wit's end. I have two daughters, one is fifteen and one is fourteen. I have a great relationship with the younger one, but the older one has stopped talking to me. She locks herself in her room all night, and is silent at family dinners, though she rolls her eyes every time I speak. It's her sixteenth birthday next month, and she refuses to have a family dinner or even a party with her friends. What can I do to get our relationship back on track?

I'm assuming you haven't had a conversation about this with your daughter yet, and you should do so. Immediately! It's so important to communicate openly with your children. Don't let your daughter think the only time you talk to her is when there's a problem.

Take her shopping or out to lunch and have the conversation. Keep it light, so it doesn't feel like an intervention. Be positive and supportive, and LISTEN to what she has to say. Don't compare her to your other daughter. She'll probably be defensive and difficult at first, but keep it relaxed and friendly. If she does open up, don't start preaching. Just keep listening. And be patient—she's only fifteen and she may not be able to fully verbalize what she's feeling.

Keep making time to talk to her, and keep a close watch on her. If she regresses or if her grades begin to slip or if she starts hanging out with a bad crowd, then you should seek professional help. Start with her guidance counselor before you go to a doctor.

The teenage years are tough. Kids don't feel like kids, but they don't yet fit into the adult world. If you give your daughter love and attention, she'll come around. Good luck!

Everybody shits on a bowl. Never allow yourself to be intimidated

I've never ever thought I was better than anyone, and I've also never thought anyone was better than me. I give credit to my dad. "Caroline," he would say, "be strong. Caroline, be smart. Caroline, don't take anybody's bullshit." And then he'd pause, and with a wave of his hand he'd close with, "Everybody shits on a bowl."

Now you can see where I get my tell-it-like-I-see-it attitude. What my dad was really saying is that no matter who a person is in their public life, whether they're a movie star, the president, or the clerk at the grocery store, we're all human. We're all equal. We all shit on a bowl. As coarse as this sounds, all it means is that we're all people, we're all equal, and you shouldn't be intimidated by anyone.

I always think of his words of wisdom before a big meeting. If I was about to meet the president of the United States, I would be cool as a cucumber. I'd remind myself that he's a person, just like me, and I'd be calm. I can go onstage in front of five thousand people, no problem. Just before I walk out there, I remind myself that each and every one of them spent some alone time in the bathroom this morning. We're all the same.

I cannot tell you how many times this little bit of wisdom from my father has saved me.

A few summers ago my husband and I took a wonderful trip to Jordan. I fell in love with the country, its exotic sights. Long story short, the Manzos ended up hanging out with the prince and princess of Jordan. (I know, sometimes I can't believe my life.)

One night I was invited to a dinner party with the princess and the prince at their palace. It was gorgeous but also very formal, and I was advised of the rules I needed to follow when interacting with His and Her Highness. I was seated next to the prince, and at the beginning of dinner I leaned over to him. "What's up?" I joked.

Everybody suddenly looked at me, in horror. But the prince just smiled widely, and we ended up having a fascinating conversation. I talked to him like I would talk to anyone else. He's just a man after all. He loved my openness, and we had the best time.

I wasn't trying to be rude or break the rules. He seemed like a nice guy and I just wanted to give him the chance to talk like a regular person. I love meeting people, and I am always polite. I shake hands well, I make eye contact, and I engage with the person immediately. But I never forget, we're all the same. We all shit on a bowl.

If I ever meet the queen of England, I'll do whatever they tell me; I'll bow, I'll curtsy. But it wouldn't be out of character for me to say, "Hey, Your Majesty, what's up?" She's Queen Elizabeth, but she's also Elizabeth who's going to go home and feed her dogs and wash her face, just like I do every night.

No matter what you've heard about a person before you meet him, whether he's famous or powerful or just someone with a reputation for anger, I believe that most people want to connect, they want to be able to relate to others and be accepted.

I've taught my kids the same thing. We saw Bill Clinton at an event recently, and they were so excited. "Go talk to him," I said. They all got nervous but I told them, "Remember, he's just like us, don't make me say it!" And they all went over and talked to him. He was so lovely, so gracious. He talked to them for about ten minutes and took pictures with them. They were all so elated after they met him—that man is living history, and he was so kind to them.

To this day, I've never been starstruck. I went to the White House Correspondents' dinner last year. It was a great experience, but I treated it just like any other dinner at The Brownstone. So what if I had George Clooney to my right, and Kate Hudson to my left? I focused on the guests at my table. I ended up sitting next to Ryan Kwanten from *True Blood*, and we had a blast, laughing and joking all night. I didn't feel like I had to run around and schmooze and get pictures with all the stars, I just wanted to enjoy myself.

What was weird that night—and is weird always—is the concept that I'm famous in any way, and that people sometimes have a hard time talking to me because they know me from TV. Fans will get all nervous when they approach me, and it blows my mind. I always want to remind them that I'm just like them, we all use the toilet, we all have bad breath, and we're all human. I get in trouble at public events because I frequently run over my time limits. But I want to make sure that if my fans cared enough to show up, they get a chance to really talk to me to know the real me. Publicists are always trying to hurry me along, but these lovely people got me here, and the least I can do is give them a decent conversation.

At the end of the day, I'm nothing special. I'm just the same Caroline I've always been. I happen to be a lucky bitch, nothing more than that. I have no talent, I don't sing, I don't dance. My face doesn't scare people, but it ain't stunning. This body is what it is at fifty-one years of age. The adoration is something I have a difficult time with. But I'll always be gracious about it. I'm grateful that you're reading my book, and I hope my show makes you laugh. But at the end of the day, I'm just like you.

Tell the truth. Lies will always bite you in the ass.

The truth is something you can never escape. It will always catch you. Truth comes from maturity and knowing who you are. I know myself. I'm five foot one and 130 pounds. I'm fifty-one and I'm wrinkly. I have very pretty eyes and a great rack—and yes, both are real; I would never lie about that, what's the point? When I started on this show, I knew they wanted drama. I also knew enough about TV to know that trying to bullshit while you have a house full of cameras recording your every move is just about the stupidest thing in the world. You tell a lie on a reality show, they're just going to run the footage of you doing the thing you deny, while you sit there and destroy your credibility. Lying makes anyone look like a fool, but being caught in a lie on a reality show makes you look so much worse.

In the years since I started on the show, there has been a string of very well documented catfights, and I have refused to be drawn into nearly all of them. The only time I reacted to the crap was at the season-one reunion, and at that time, I only got angry because what was being discussed was destructive to my parents. They're off limits.

Ever since then, I have steered clear of all the catfights that the public seem to love. I don't need to get involved. Frankly, on the show and in real life, my policy is to never engage with a liar. If you are distorting the truth to serve yourself, that's your problem, not mine. Say anything you want, true or not. I will weather the storm. I will take the beating, but I will never fight back. I will never honor the lie with a response. I think that my character speaks louder than that. I know my truth, and I know whatever that truth is will eventually come out.

BEHIND THE SCENES

Reunion shows are incredibly draining, and they take forever to tape. The first year, it took us eight hours to cover a season that was only six episodes long. Ever since, we've shot for between ten and twelve hours. We have breaks, of course—we stop to eat, and we can get our makeup retouched if we cry—but these shoots are tough. There are no rules, anything and everything is fair game once the cameras start rolling. It's stressful, and I'm always glad that Jacqueline is there with me—an ally is the most important accessory at a reunion show! No matter how much I prepare, Andy loves to throw curveballs at a reunion. So far, I'm lucky that he hasn't really been able to spring anything on me, but that doesn't mean he won't at some point. There are no words for how exhausted I am at the end of a reunion taping. I usually just have a quiet dinner with Al, and he calms me down.

I have seen lies go bad. I've seen them destroy marriages, families, and lives. It's never worth it in the end. So I don't mind keeping my distance from a lie. I'll take the momentary public humiliation, because I know at the end of the day, I'll be fine. But when a lie comes around and hits the liar, it hits them hard.

I'm not going to pretend the lies don't bother me. Just because I choose not to address them, doesn't mean I'm not boiling inside. The most annoying thing is to be sitting across from someone who is lying to your face, and you know it. This happens a lot on the reunion shows. I will always give a liar every opportunity to come clean. I try to bring the conversation around to an opportunity for them to make things right. But if they continue to stick with the false story, it makes me very, very angry, or more accurately, very frustrated. There's something amazing about people who are guilty. They yell. They scream. They need to convince. When someone is not lying, they talk calmly. There's no guilt. Guilty people need an audience, they need theatrics, to make themselves believable.

My first impulse when a liar starts to scream and defend him- or herself is to set things straight. To tell the liar I know they're lying, that they're a terrible person for lying, and how dare they? But I hold back. Even when it's someone who habitually lies to me, I realize that they're never going to change. I follow my own advice, I disengage, I nod my head and I walk away. I have bigger fish to fry.

I don't have a poker face. When someone's lying to me, my face lets them know that I'm not stupid. I know exactly what they're doing. You've probably seen this face on TV. I can't hide it. My body language is stupidly blunt. It takes a lot for me to turn you off. But

Ask Caroline

Caroline: I had a falling-out with my best friend a few years ago. We've recently reconnected, and I would like to invite her to my family events. Due to the nature of our fallout I'm concerned that not everyone in my family will let bygones be bygones and welcome her back to the fold. What would be the best way to approach my concerns with my friend and my family members?

Baby steps! First of all, if you found forgiveness in your heart and want to have this person in your life again, that's your choice. I'm a little curious to know what the falling-out was about, since you feel like your family will be against a reconciliation. Not knowing the situation, all I can suggest is that you sit down with your family members and tell them how you feel and why you want to move forward with the relationship. Listen to what they have to say with an open mind and know that they are coming from a place of love and concern. Talk it out rationally.

I would also let your friend know that there may be issues. How she handles it will be an indication of where her mind-set is on the relationship as well. Your friend should want to move along in a proactive way and understand that there may be some crow to eat.

Once you get past these little hurdles, proceed with caution and just enjoy yourselves, build on the good times and leave the bad in the past.

Relationships are never easy, but those that are willing to fight for them are keepers. Good luck.

you will know I turned you off, and in your heart and soul you'll know why I did it. You'll know I can see through you.

I've seen a lot in my lifetime, and I've seen a lot of good people do stupid things. I've seen a lot of heartbreaking situations over an untruth, and it was never worth it. I always tell my children the truth, and sometimes the truth hurts. But I want the same honesty in return. Don't spare my feelings, you're not doing me any favors.

Lies push people to the point of no return, and some lies are so bad you can never come back from them. I'd rather deal with the truth that hurts for ten minutes than deal with a lie for a lifetime.

I may not be the smartest or the prettiest, but you will remember me.

I am smart but I'm not the smartest. I'm not unattractive, but I'm not the prettiest. But, trust me, you'll remember me.

When I engage in conversation with you, I'm all yours. If you're going to take the time to have lunch or dinner with me, then the least I can do is give you my full attention. It's a matter of respect, simple as that.

It's almost a disservice to me that I've become known through the show as an opinionated person. Sure, I have a lot to say, but I also love to listen to people. You can learn a lot by listening. Listen between the lines. Sometimes people want your help, or your understanding, but the full truth is too hard for them to say. So listen well, and listen intuitively.

It's funny, as much as I don't love being interviewed, when I am sitting talking to someone, even a complete stranger, I find myself asking question after question. I want to learn more about people. What makes them tick? What motivates them? I've never been to a therapist, ever. I haven't ever felt like I needed one. But I've been told that sometimes I act like one.

I'm sure this is a direct result of being the middle kid in a big family. There were the older kids, the younger kids, and then there was me, stuck in the middle of both.

I learned early on it was better to listen, and keep quiet. I read the situation and acted accordingly. I never found myself taking sides; instead I was able to develop good friendships with all of my siblings, for the most part.

It wasn't until I was an adult that I learned to engage with other adults. As a child, I was painfully shy to the point of complete silence. I definitely didn't make a splash as a kid. But as an adult, I got my sea legs. I realized I had opinions, and I became unafraid to share them. And it just grew from there. But being opinionated was secondary to the importance I placed on truly listening to others, working to understand them and learning from them. That's what makes me memorable.

BEHIND THE SCENES

We have absolutely no control over what makes it onto the air. Sometimes you'll film a scene that you're proud of, and when the episode comes along, it's missing. I shot a scene that I was proud of with Lauren during her weight loss struggle in season four. She was frustrated with the person she saw in the mirror, and I told her about the Lauren that the world sees—a cute, brave girl with a great sense of humor and a wonderful boyfriend who loves her very much. I was heartbroken when it ended up on the cutting-room floor, because it gave really good context to the rest of her weight struggle. But at the end of the day, we just have to have faith in our producers—they have done such a great job so far.

I wish I was funnier. I love it when someone can just be the life of the party, swing from the chandeliers, make everybody laugh. That's a true gift. It's just not one of my gifts.

(On the flip side, I hate it when people do stupid or contrived things just to get attention. Through my life experiences and my time on the show, I've encountered my fair share of people who hurt others so that they can get attention. People who make themselves feel better at the expense of another can go to hell. They're not worth a glance in their direction; they mean nothing to me.)

I just hope at the end of this journey, people remember me as someone who always had integrity, and stuck to her beliefs. If it works out that in five years, nobody remembers me at all, I'm fine with that. I'll still make my mark on the people that I meet.

You have only one life. Take that stage and own it.

I've seen so many people die before their time, and it always breaks my heart. I wonder what their last thoughts were, and what their regrets were. For a relatively unadventurous girl from Queens, I've already had a remarkable life, and that has come from being ready to step up when a good opportunity comes my way.

I don't seek adventure. I was perfectly happy as an anonymous wife and mother.

I was hesitant to do the show. I'm not a big TV person. But I figured I would audition for kicks, a summer diversion, a laugh, and nothing would come of it. I never thought I'd get cast. But when I got the job, I took a leap and said yes. I wanted to see where the adventure would take me. I wanted to set an example for my kids, and one day my grandkids—you should always jump at any opportunity presented to you. Once we were done filming the first season, there was a gap of time until what we shot hit the air. As the premiere date got closer and closer, I started to get really nervous. Albert swooped in to save the day and took me on a vacation when that first half-hour teaser aired. We went down to Florida and spent the week on a friend's boat. I watched that first episode on a boat in the middle of the ocean all alone with my husband, and to this day, when I get the DVD of an upcoming episode, I wait until I can watch it with Al.

Even now, five years later, this show puts me outside my comfort zone. It has caused me tremendous heartbreak, and I've had powerful moments of regret over the show. But there have been amazing highs too—and that makes me so glad I took the leap of faith. You only live once.

I get asked all the time what's the best thing that came out of the show. And I always think of the same two things. The first was sharing with viewers Albie's learning disability. It was his decision to share that. While we were filming, he received the letter notifying him that he failed law school—he missed his grade by 87/100th of a point. He came so close to realizing his life's dream, without any help, all while dealing with the challenges of a learning disorder. Albie agreed to let the cameras follow that journey. Even now, when I revisit those episodes, I nearly die. But through it, Albie became a role model for others who were struggling just like he had.

The second best thing the show has given me is a far cry from the first. Now don't laugh, but my husband never asks for anything, so when the show enabled us to visit the Playboy Mansion and he had a chance to meet Hef, I've never seen him more excited. When we visited, Hef was initially not receiving any guests. But I knew how badly Albert wanted to meet him, so I went and started asking around. After about a half hour of my persistence, we were invited inside, and lo and behold, Hef came downstairs and greeted us. The smile on Al's face was something I'll treasure forever, and it was a direct result of me taking the chance to do this TV show.

BEHIND THE SCENES

People always ask me why I'm acting weird in the scene where Albie tells me he failed law school. The whole crew was sitting to my left, on a staircase, filming the scene. As Albie started to tell me, his cheeks began to turn red. Ever since he was little, this flush meant he was about to cry. So as he kept talking, I was glaring at the crew, begging them with my eyes to stop the cameras. I didn't want them to film him crying. But I'm glad they kept the cameras running, this is probably my favorite scene ever in the show.

While it's still hard for me to wrap my head around how the show has made me into somewhat of a public figure, I am very thankful that it allows me to do some good too. I've visited people in the hospital, complete strangers who've written to me. When I talk to them and they say my words help them find a way out of their depression, I feel proud and honored. Young kids tell me that because of me they've been able to come out to their parents. Women tell me that because of me they've had the strength to leave their husbands. Somehow, my life on TV has helped guide some people, and that is beyond my wildest dreams. If I can help a stranger, even a little bit, then it makes my decision to do the show one of the best I've ever made.

It's impossible to know if every opportunity is worth your time. But you know what? You'll never know if you don't try, so if something feels right, do it. And if it works, great. If not, pick yourself up, dust yourself off, and start over again. That's life.

Ask Caroline

Dear Caroline: I work from home on my own business, but people tend to underestimate me. How do I let them know that my work is serious business without being obnoxious?

Why do you feel the need to prove yourself to anyone? If you are happy and secure in what you do then that's all that matters.

Very simply put, if the work is getting done and you are maintaining a schedule that is proactive where the phones are getting answered and clients are being serviced, who's better than you? You have flexibility with your time and money, and that sounds like a win/win to me.

Lay out the pros and cons: you have no travel expense, you have no overhead such as office rent and utilities, you have peace of mind and can focus rather than get caught up in water-cooler gossip, you don't have to worry about anyone borrowing your stapler and never returning it, your hours are your own, you can write off your work space on your taxes, you can save money on office attire, and people don't understand why you do it? Pshhht—you sound like a winner to me.

Albie: in his own words

I was eleven or twelve when I was told that I had a learning disorder. I didn't even suspect that I had one, but I guess my teachers suspected something. They put me through a battery of tests, from math to puzzles to reading, and when the results came through, I was classified as having a disability. From that moment on, everything changed. I felt different, and being moved to remedial classes only made it worse. Even though I was mainly struggling with reading comprehension, I was given an assistant teacher to help with all my classes, and I hated it. All the kids gave me flak for the extra help I was receiving.

I didn't think I was different from anyone else. Sure it took me two or three times longer to understand something that I read, but that was it. The only reason I knew I was different was that somebody told me.

As an adult, I've learned to deal with my disorder. I don't like to use e-mails or texts for communication; I prefer to talk either in person or over the phone. When I am reading, I have to concentrate so hard that I can be completely oblivious to what's going on around me. If you come into a room and talk to me while I'm reading, I won't remember a word you say. I have a visual processing disorder, and now that I've learned how to work with it, it's really not that big of a deal. I'm not trying to downplay it at all, but compared to other afflictions people in this world have, it's not that bad.

My experiences at college were wonderful. Fordham was so accommodating to me. I was determined

(continued)

that the stigma that had ruined high school would not transfer to college. On my first day at Fordham, I handed over an envelope outlining my disorder to a professor, and from then everything was taken care of. Nobody knew I had a learning disability. When time came for exams, I was quietly taken out of class to a separate room to take the test. They had assistants that I could use, but they were on a side of the campus that was hard to get to. It was easy to manage my learning disability without anyone knowing that I had one.

For the first year of college, I was reluctant to take advantage of this assistance. I wanted to do it by myself, but as I started to hit speed bumps, I started to use the learning aides they offered.

I remember that as soon as I got my book list for the first year of college, my mom said that she was going to go and buy herself the same books, and she would do my homework with me every week. We'd read the assignment and then we'd work on the homework. It was really an amazing thing that she did, and it was a time that we became really close as adults. That was a huge help, and it gave me a lot of confidence. Eventually I stopped relying on Mom and also on the other assistance that Fordham offered, and I was proud to complete college on my own.

I always wanted to be a lawyer. I interned at an amazing law firm in New York City, starting my junior year in college. I was the youngest guy there, and I loved it. I realized I wanted to become a lawyer, so I started practicing for the LSAT (the entrance exam you need to take to get into law school), and again, the

(continued)

reading part kicked my ass. You only have thirty-five minutes to read the reading section. I knew I was going to get into trouble with it. I spent a lot of energy, time, and money prepping to pass the LSAT, and when I did it was a huge accomplishment. Law school was insanely tough. There was nobody there to back me up, but what was I going to do? It was a chance I had to take, even though I knew the odds were stacked against me.

When I failed out, I was .087 below the curve. It was a scary time for me. I could tell I was starting to fall behind. The writing was on the wall for me to fail out.

I'm a private person, but I'm not ashamed of anything I do. You can't be choosy about what makes it on air and what doesn't. When I got that letter, telling me I failed out of school, I knew it was going to be tough, but I also knew I had to show it on air. I knew the letter was coming, but actually receiving it, holding it in my hands, made it all real. In the back of my mind, I was thinking, "One day, I'll want to watch this clip, I'll want to show my kids what I went through."

The hard part about doing this show is you have to go through everything twice. You go through things as they happen, and you relive them when they air a year later. It can be draining to get past a difficult experience, and then you have to rehash it in public months later. Even now, writing this, I'm reliving that time.

I felt like I failed out for a second time when the episode finally aired. The media did not understand it. They framed it like I failed my GED, instead of failing out of one of the top law schools in the country. They talked

(continued)

about me like I was an idiot. To this day, if you Google me, the top news story that comes up is titled "Albie Manzo May Be Slow But He's Determined." It hurts and makes me angry, but you have to let these things go. I still have the letter informing me that I failed out. Soon after receiving it I signed it and I wrote, "Thanks for everything, Albie Manzo" and one day when I'm on the cover of Forbes, I'll send it back to that school and show them that I made it anyway.

I love what I'm doing now with our beverage company BLK. My mom has always told us that life takes you in a million directions at a million miles an hour, and it's tough for anybody to make plans for the future. Your life can change in a phone call. I think that BLK is what I was supposed to be doing. Working with my brother and my uncle and cousins is exactly where I was supposed to end up.

We now own one of the fastest growing beverage companies in the country, and it's going to be very successful. By the time I'm done, I'll be saying that getting kicked out of law school was the best thing that ever happened to me. And you will have seen that whole journey on TV, and any viewers with a learning disability will see that you can do anything, no matter who tells you that you can't!

I gauge my problems with one question: Will this affect my life one year from now? If the answer is yes, I solve it. If the answer is no, I don't obsess over it.

I've lived with this motto for as long as I can remember. It is the best way to dig your way out of the small problems that crop up daily in our lives, and it can be even more powerful advice when you've got some major drama on your table.

In April of last year, Lauren was opening Cafface, and I was her backer. I invested all my money into launching the store with her. I called it the college fund she never used. And just before the store opened, when we didn't know if it was going to work, I had to live with the fact that I'd just sunk a quarter million dollars, all of my personal savings, into a start-up business.

I knew I was taking a big risk. So I asked myself what would the problem be in a year, and I got my answer. In a year, if the business tanked, I'd lose a ton of money, but much worse, my daughter's heart would be broken. This answer helped me assess the situation and deal with it in the present, redirecting my energy to what was really important. I realized that if I lost the money, I could always make it back. I could do another season of the show. I could start another business venture. But what was more important was protecting Lauren; it would be harder for her to come back from such a disappointment.

So I threw everything I had at Cafface—I made sure I went in there every day and devoted my life to it. Suddenly I was fighting to save my daughter from a broken heart. I had a goal, and my worries about the money and all the stuff attached to it all just eased up.

Ask Caroline

Dear Mrs. Manzo, My fourteen-year-old daughter is becoming very difficult to talk to. She's barely passing at school, she's talking back to her teachers, and she has developed an awful attitude problem. This is causing our two younger daughters to copy her, and it's making my husband and I argue a lot. What can I do? I feel like I've tried everything.

Wow, it sounds like you do have your hands full. First, identify if there is a specific incident that caused your daughter to act this way. Seek counseling either through her school or your own physician. Once you figure out the root of her problem, you'll be able to start dealing with her in a way that will help her.

Please never argue with your husband in front of the kids. If you disagree with each other, talk it out behind closed doors. If you're just frustrated and snappy, try to keep it under control. If you are still angry ten minutes later, take him aside and talk in private.

Your husband and you need to take back control of the house. Set rules and curfews, and enforce them. If you ground them for two days, make sure that's how long they stay grounded.

No one ever said parenting was easy. Dig in, hold tight, and keep your eyes on the goal. Don't be ashamed to ask for help, and don't blame yourself. Stay united with your husband, and help your daughter back into a positive state of mind. Keep the faith, and good luck.

That business was a game changer for Lauren, it was make-or-break. And we made it.

Your daughter breaks up with her boyfriend and she's sixteen? He cheated on her and she can't go to the prom? That's not a big deal. Take her out for pizza, let her cry. I didn't go to the prom either and I'm still alive.

But if your daughter is cutting herself, drop everything in your life and deal with it. For the record, Lauren never cut herself, but that's a perfect example of something that in a year will only worsen. Don't panic, don't freak out, just be there for that kid and make sure she's getting every bit of help she needs and that she has your total support to get her through it.

A lot of parents I know are lenient on their kids when it comes to drugs. I'm not because I consider drugs a problem with consequences that could hang around for a year and even longer. Your husband forgets an anniversary? Are you going to still care in a year? No. Give him a hard time for five minutes and then make him take you someplace nice and try to save the night.

But what if you find out that he's cheating on you? It's a problem right now, and how you handle it will affect your life a year from now. I know it's every woman's worst nightmare, and I'm lucky beyond words that I've never had to face it. But if I did, I'll tell you one thing: I wouldn't lose my mind and scream and call him names and kick him out. I'd sit my husband down and ask him, "What's broken?"

I'm not talking about a long-term affair or finding out your husband is a serial cheater. I'm talking about your normally good husband who slipped up once. You need to find out what's broken and how to fix it now, because if you married a good man who made just one mistake, you'll probably get through it, and a year from now you'll be back on track.

Women who talk obsessively about their weight drive me crazy. You've gained twenty pounds over the winter? So what. Lose ten and make yourself look the best you can. Don't make yourself miserable and drag down everyone around you, a few extra pounds is not going to change your life. Do what's in your power and make yourself as pretty as you can at whatever weight you can get to. Your weight isn't going to impact your life in a major way a year from now. It's a yo-yo, and it's a fact of modern life. Deal with it quietly.

Each moment in your life has cause and effect. What's the cause and what's the effect of taking action or doing nothing? Ask yourself that, and you'll know whether you need to worry or not. It'll help you keep the gray hairs at bay, and you'll sleep a lot easier, trust me.

Reading will set you free.

No matter how crazy my life has ever gotten, I have always made time to read, to retreat into a book, every day. I love to read, it's my meditation, my salvation, and my recreation. I find great peace in reading.

Some of my earliest happy memories are of my mother taking my siblings and me to the library. My mother never drove, and when I was born (her sixth child), she was twenty-four. We lived in Maspeth, New York, at the time, and there was a library about six blocks from the house. Every Tuesday morning she'd round up whoever was home from school, she'd hold our hands like ducks in a row, and she'd walk us all to the library where she'd read to us.

The first books I fell in love with were the Beatrix Potter books. I read about those little rabbits and animals and just marveled at their adventures. Every week, Mom would let us all borrow two books, and the next Tuesday, we'd all march back and return them.

I still read as often as I can. I could read a five-hundred-page book in a night. I'll read history, comedy, or biographies. I love to learn things, and there's nothing more thrilling to me than a good historical novel.

My favorite book of all time is *Gone with the Wind*. Even though it's pure fiction, I still love going into Scarlett O'Hara's world and being amazed at how she views life. There's something so exciting about sharing someone's journey in a book. I get so lost in that new world, I can see and hear and feel it around me. It's intoxicating.

I wish Albert, Lauren, and Albie liked reading books, but they don't. They'll read magazines or blogs, but that's just not the same to me. I don't like magazines; I prefer a good book I can sink my teeth into.

I have always thought of my books as my friends. Though now I carry my NOOK ereader with me on flights to save my back from lugging a heavy load, I still love the feel of a book, the weight and smell of the paper. When I got this opportunity to write a book for you all, I was so honored. The whole time I was writing it, I was aware that the little girl who used to go to the library with her mother, and marvel at all the books, would soon have her own book in that library.

I will always be grateful for this opportunity, and to each and every one of you who are reading this right now. Life is a crazy ride, and I could never have dreamed that one day, I would get the chance to be an author. I don't know how successful this book will be, or

Caroline's all-time favorite reads

1. *Gone with the Wind*—Margaret Mitchell
2. *White Oleander*—Janet Fitch
3. *The Help*—Kathryn Stockett
4. *The Client*—John Grisham
5. *Defending Jacob*—William Landay
6. *The Glass Castle*—Jeannette Walls
7. *The Girl with the Dragon Tattoo*—Stieg Larsson
8. *The Da Vinci Code*—Dan Brown
9. *The Red Tent*—Anita Diamant
10. *The Bluest Eye*—Toni Morrison

whether you'll love it or hate it, but it's been a project so near and dear to my heart that I will always be amazed when I hold this book in my hands. And for that, I thank you.

Respect is free, but you gotta earn your keep.

True respect is possibly the greatest thing in the world. It is love, it's admiration, and it's something that you build over time by being a good person. And once you have it, you are responsible for living up to the respect that you were given. It's powerful and it's amazing. You can never assume that someone will respect you just because of who you are, and you can never take it for granted once you get it. Just because you gave birth doesn't make you a mother. Just because you impregnated someone doesn't make you a father. You have to earn that respect. I don't expect you to respect me. I'm happy to work for it.

I've been forced to really think about respect since I got cast on the *Real Housewives*. My life has been exposed to millions of people, and now my life is considered to be public property. For the most part, I've been treated with respect. I've been lucky. But of course there are some assholes out there.

BEHIND THE SCENES

I love filming the interview segments. We probably shoot one every two weeks when we are in production, which means we have already shot the scenes and the editors are piecing the footage together to make the episodes. The producers arrive at my house armed with pages of questions, and it's just me, talking to a producer for eight or nine hours straight. We get hair and makeup when we film these interviews (we also get hair and makeup for the reunion shows), so it feels a bit more glamorous. Don't get me wrong—as much fun as these segments are, they can also be draining. You go from laughter to tears and back again. But I love them because it's just me, reacting and telling the truth. Nobody is trying to mess with me! Filming these segments is the only time I feel free and truly comfortable when we are shooting the show.

I stopped reading online comments after season one. A coward behind a computer doesn't bother me at all. It's pointless to empower a stranger who is trying to hurt you. I realize they don't truly know me—if I saw them on the street, I wouldn't recognize them. So their comments don't mean anything to me. I have never looked for respect from people who don't know me, so once I started on the show, I was in good shape to deal with the slings and arrows.

My viewers, on the other hand, matter to me, a lot. Their respect means the world to me. They're the reason I'm here. They're the reason I'm writing this book. Even though Bravo put out a great television show, the fans are the ones that keep it going, and for that, I respect and appreciate them.

My goal on this show is to be able to get to the end of it with respect from the viewers still intact. That was one of the first things I told myself when I found out I got the job on *Real Housewives*. Anything I do in front of a camera lives forever, any behavior, any damn stupid brain fart, lives forever on the Internet. So from the very start, I promised myself I'd keep my cool and never resort to any sort of regrettable name-calling. As tough as it has gotten, I think I've done OK.

I blew my cool at the first-season reunion, because my family was being attacked. I was also very inexperienced, and that was the first time we'd sat down as a panel, and obviously, the questions were designed to get us to react. I hated that I lost my temper, and I hated it that people saw me that way. I was frustrated and angry. As soon as I calmed down, I vowed to myself to never be that easily manipulated again. Sometimes the best way to respect yourself and others is to shut your mouth completely.

I maintain silence out of respect for myself. Like Popeye says, I yam what I yam, and that's all that I yam. Quite frankly, when all is said and done, when this fifteen minutes is up, I'm going to turn around and look at the four faces I love more than anything in the world and say, "What do you want for dinner?" I know who I am. I don't need to prove myself to anybody. I am confident that my legacy from this show will be positive and respectful.

I'm Albert's wife, and Albie, Christopher, and Lauren's mom, but I never forgot who Caroline Manzo is.

It might surprise people who don't know me too well, but as much as being a wife and a mother is my life, I consider myself Caroline Manzo first, wife and mother second. The other titles are great, but they aren't the girl I was born.

I have clung to my individuality through thick and thin. And I think this is one of the greatest success secrets I ever stumbled upon. I believe that staying true to myself has been the key to a long, happy marriage, and it has made my kids stronger and happier. It has given me a great moral compass, and it has given me confidence in all kinds of circumstances.

In love, the most important thing for me is to always remain the same girl that Al fell in love with. When Al looks at me these days, he tells me he sees the nineteen-year-old me that he fell for. This doesn't mean I'm acting like some crazy celebutante or dressing like a kid, it just means that I still have the same energy and heart that I have had all my life.

On the day that all the kids are finally out of the house, the last thing I would ever want is for Albert to look at me and see a stranger. I think that happens to a lot of couples; they have been so focused on kids, career, and life that they just let themselves drift apart.

It hasn't always been easy. There were times when I lost touch with myself. Life got on top of me and things got hard. After three kids in three years, I gave up. The last thing I could think of was putting on makeup or high heels. I had always had long hair until I got pregnant with Christopher. I got so sick of having to deal with it, I chopped it off. I let go of all the things in my life that made me

Ways to make time for yourself in a busy life

1. Take a class at a local college. Study something that interests you, whether it's art or history or learning a second language.

2. Join a group, like a book club or a scrapbooking club, ceramics, painting. Bounce off other people in a creative environment.

3. Enroll in a gym and take classes. You'll always feel better if you've exercised, and the benefit is that you'll also look better.

4. Find a quiet corner in your house and make it your own to read, knit, write, or do whatever you like to do at home.

5. Go to a park and sit on a bench by yourself. Feel the breeze and the sun on your face. Watch kids play and do some good people-watching.

Caroline. I lost myself in a mix of exhaustion and apathy, and I just didn't care anymore.

It was a huge trap and I fell into it, time and time again. Sometimes for a month, sometimes just for a day or a week. And then I'd see myself in a mirror and gasp. I'd realize I was being Mommy, and not Caroline. I'd snap myself out of it and do whatever it took to get everything back on track.

When I was pregnant with Christopher I got my real estate license, and that was something that I did just for me. On top of giving me my own income—so I could buy my own Keds sneakers, the must-have for every woman of the 1990s—it gave me a reason to put on lipstick and heels, get out of the house, and meet people. It gave me a great sense of self-worth, which felt even better when I was able to put Albie through Fordham with the money I made selling real estate. My husband could have paid for it, but it was something that I wanted to do. I bought Lauren her first car. These things gave me such a sense of accomplishment. I was proud of myself.

Keeping in touch with yourself in the middle of motherhood isn't easy, but it's crucial. Where there's a will, there's a way, and you'll be a better mother for it.

There's always someone out there who's got it worse than you. Say a prayer and help them.

We live in the best country in the world. We have so much to be grateful for. And one thing that drives me crazy, is people who complain nonstop about problems that aren't that significant. You see it all the time on Facebook—"Worst. Day. Ever!" someone will post, usually because she spilled her coffee or got stuck in traffic.

I just shake my head. Somebody lost a child today, somebody found out she had cancer today. Somewhere on this Earth, thousands of people are fighting for their lives, right now. There's a growing sense of entitlement in this country, with people expecting everything to be perfect for them, and if anything isn't, people are always so quick to blame others. Newsflash: that's not the way it works. You're losing your mind because you put shoes on hold at the mall and they sold them? Big deal. Get a grip. You're blessed if that's your biggest worry.

BEHIND THE SCENES

"Happy Birthday to You" is the most expensive song to use on a TV show—they have to pay rights to air a song—which means that if you're filming a birthday scene, your friends and family aren't allowed to sing happy birthday to you. It sounds like a small sacrifice, and in many ways it is. But there's no getting around the fact that hearing any other song on your birthday is just plain weird, and it makes your birthday feel less special. I don't think I'll be filming many more birthdays, because I love it when my family sings "Happy Birthday to You" to me!

People assume that I'm wealthy, that I never had a hard time of anything, but this couldn't be further from the truth. There were times we couldn't afford diapers for the kids. When I was pregnant with Albie, we couldn't afford maternity clothes, so I just wore sweats or leggings and Al's shirts every day. That winter, I sported this big old bomber jacket I'd bought Al years before. His mother wanted to take me out and buy me a "proper winter coat," but I was happy wearing his big old coat.

I remember at our poorest, I fell in love with an Esprit blouse at Bamberger's. The damn thing was just a simple striped shirt, and it was $35. I knew we couldn't afford it, but that never stopped me from looking at it every time I was in the store. That Christmas, Al's mom got me the shirt as a surprise.

The lean years have made me very aware of how important it is to keep your perspective when things get tough. No matter how bad things are, somebody else always has it much worse. When we started to have some money and we moved to Franklin Lakes, I made sure to always be involved in the local charities, and find ways to help others. One thing that I love about where I live is that the people of Franklin Lakes are generous and kind. It's heartening to find that in an affluent community.

Life is short and the cards are dealt randomly. The older I get, the more grateful I am at the end of every day when I still have my family and loved ones around me. I am starting to feel blessed just for making it through each day.

It's not all roses, I'm not gonna lie. Some days are tougher than others. On a bad day, I will find a way to just drop out for a minute. I'll go to my bedroom, or I'll go take a drive around the neighborhood. The streets of New York are great for me to get lost in and do

Random acts of kindness

You don't need to go work in a soup kitchen to prove you're a good person who understands what's really important in life. Sometimes just shifting your attitude toward those around you is equally as effective. Smile at that stranger. Who knows, that smile might have made the day of someone who is having a rough go at life. Give up your seat on the bus, it's not gonna kill you. If you see someone's parking meter expire, throw a quarter in. Help someone with a stroller up the stairs on the subway. There's always somebody who can benefit from your kindness.

some thinking and get on top of what's bringing me down and clear my head. I regain my perspective and remind myself I'm so lucky; things aren't that bad.

Something good happens every day. During these moments of reflection take a minute to dig a bit deeper and be grateful. So think twice before you throw a tantrum about breaking a nail or losing your phone. Think of how bad things could truly be. Can you imagine being told you have two months to live? If you did, that's heartbreaking. It's serious. If you didn't, then shut up!

Caroline's ways to give back

I've always been involved with charities, and here are three of my favorites. You can easily find a charity that touches your heart for personal reasons if you want to get involved in helping others. You also don't have to join a charity to make a difference—if you know of someone in your life who needs help, be that person to help. Affecting one life can mean just as much as working for a charity.

The Wounded Warrior Project: No one should be treated with more honor than those who go fight for our country, and unfortunately so many of our warriors return wounded. When they come back they need our help.

Best Friends Animal Sanctuary: This nationwide pet adoption charity is all about saving the lives of animals. I've always had dogs and cats and pets, and I love working to get these dogs adopted.

Autism Speaks: This charity is very close to my heart because we have children in our family with autism.

Afterword

I've tried to give you a clear picture of who I am, and hopefully you now have a better understanding of me and the rules I live my life by. I hope you got a few laughs out of it, and maybe figured out how to solve a problem or two in your own life.

I've shared a lot more than you would ordinarily see on the show, because I've been able to speak to you in my own words, from my own mouth.

I still chose to keep a lot of my private life private, and I hope you're OK with that. Some things have to remain the private possessions of my family. The feuds with various cast mates will continue to be addressed in upcoming seasons, and that's the appropriate place for them. They didn't need to be addressed here. It's been a very difficult tightrope to walk in terms of what I will allow the show to film, and which aspects of my life I want them to show on TV. It's been even more intense during the process of writing this book. I've been driven to talk about things, such as the loss of my father-in-law, that are deeply personal and still carry a lot of hurt with them.

It was an interesting process to be writing this book at the same time as our most difficult season was airing. Season four was filmed directly following season three. We normally have an eight-month break between seasons, but that time we just went right into the next season. This meant that season four was filmed a year before it aired. I was miserable for most of the season. I resented being forced into situations I'd rather avoid with people I didn't want to associate with. It was painful to be reminded of just how much I did not enjoy that season, and to have to relive it.

My own advice in this book helped me deal with a lot of the frustrations that came from watching how this fourth season played out on-screen. It also helped me get my head straight for the fourth-season reunion show, which I'd been dreading. I took my own advice, and it worked! I was positive, confident, and I stuck to my guns.

You're probably sick of reading this, but I'm going to say it one last time: I'm just a housewife; I'm just a mom. I'm a regular woman who lives in New Jersey and I've been catapulted out into the world. I pray that in at least a small way, reading this book has made a difference in your life.

The main thing I'd love you to take away from reading this book is that you can do it too. You can do anything I can do. You can make a change in your life, or somebody else's. You don't have to be on television; you don't have to be famous. You just have to care. You can do it in your own home, you can do it on the block where you live, or you can do it on a bigger scale. If your own life experiences can permit you to help someone going through the same situation, then do it.

Now that you've read about my journey, I also hope you're thinking, holy shit, if she can do it, so can I. I'm living proof that anything is possible. At forty-six years of age I completely turned my life around, and at fifty-one I wrote my first book. If you have a goal, and it's in your heart and you have the desire and you stand strong, you can make it happen. If you fail the first time, pick yourself up and start again. Make your life happen on your own terms and take control of your future.

I don't know what the universe has in store for me. I took a leap of faith five years ago, and began a very wild ride. My future is still unwritten. I have no agenda, but I'm going to be as open to new things as I was to this show when it came along. I'm perfectly happy with everything that is going on in my life right now, and I'm excited to see what my next chapters are. Whether it's more TV, another book, Al's retirement, or my first grandchild, I'm excited and I'm ready to grab that next brass ring, no matter what.

This has been the most amazing experience of my life. Through all the heartache and the tears and the frustration, the laughter and the anger, I have absolutely no regrets. One day I will look back at this experience and say, "Wow, that was one hell of a ride." I did that ride with my kids and my husband and I loved it. Thanks for coming on the ride with me.

Affirmations

I love affirmations. Every time I read one that touches me, I print it out and pin it to a corkboard in my office. I look at that board all the time, and I find endless inspiration in these sentences. I hope you like them too!

My thoughts are under my control.

You gotta love livin', baby, 'cause dyin' is a pain in the ass.

—*Frank Sinatra*

Critics don't bother me because if I do badly, I know I'm bad before they even write it. And if I'm good, I know I'm good. I know best about myself, so a critic doesn't anger me.   —*Frank Sinatra*

Happiness is an attitude. We either make ourselves miserable, or happy and strong. The amount of work is the same.

—*Francesca Reigler*

There is nothing wrong with making mistakes. Just don't respond with encores.

Don't let yourself forget what it's like to be sixteen.

If you really do put a small value upon yourself, rest assured that the world will not raise your price.

AFFIRMATIONS

Every tomorrow has two handles. We can take hold of it by the handle of anxiety, or by the handle of faith.

Don't let what you can't do interfere with what you can do.

We come to love not by finding a perfect person, but by learning to see an imperfect person perfectly.

I love people who make me laugh. I honestly think it's the thing I like most, to laugh. It cures a multitude of ills. It's probably the most important thing in a person. —*Audrey Hepburn*

Nothing is impossible, the word itself says "I'm possible."
                                        —*Audrey Hepburn*

We have to dare to be ourselves, however frightening or strange that self may prove to be. —*May Sarton*

But better to be hurt by the truth than comforted with a lie.
                                        —*Khaled Hosseini*

Life's under no obligation to give us what we expect.
                                        —*Margaret Mitchell*

Give thanks for what you are now, and keep fighting for what you want to be tomorrow. —*Fernanda Miramontes-Landeros*

Enjoy when you can, and endure when you must.
                                —*Johann Wolfgang von Goethe*

The three great essentials to achieve anything worthwhile are, first, hard work; second, stick-to-itiveness; third, common sense.
                                        —*Thomas Edison*

When you lose, don't lose the lesson.

AFFIRMATIONS

Do not worry if you have built your castles in the air. They are where they should be. Now put the foundations under them.

—Henry David Thoreau

That's the best revenge of all: happiness. Nothing drives people crazier than seeing someone have a good fucking life.

—Chuck Palahniuk

If you believe in yourself, have dedication and pride and never quit, you'll be a winner.

—Paul Bryant

Life is full of surprises and serendipity. Being open to unexpected turns in the road is an important part of success. If you try to plan every step, you may miss those wonderful twists and turns. Just find your next adventure—do it well, enjoy it—and then, not now, think about what comes next.

—Condoleezza Rice

Life is like one big Mardi Gras. But instead of showing your boobs, show people your brain, and if they like what they see, you'll have more beads than you know what to do with.

—Ellen DeGeneres

Sometimes life is going to hit you in the head with a brick. Don't lose faith.

—Steve Jobs

If it doesn't feel right, don't do it. That's the lesson. That lesson alone will save you a lot of grief. Even doubt means don't.

—Oprah Winfrey

If you have made mistakes, even serious ones, there is always another chance for you. What we call failure is not the falling down but the staying down.

—Mary Pickford

Success isn't permanent, and failure isn't fatal.

—Mike Ditka

AFFIRMATIONS

We laugh a lot. That's for sure. Sure beats the alternative, doesn't it?

—*Betty White*

Laughter gives us distance. It allows us to step back from an event, deal with it and then move on.

—*Bob Newhart*

Natural ability without education has more often raised a man to glory and virtue than education without natural ability.

—*Marcus Tullius Cicero*

[Kids] don't remember what you try to teach them. They remember what you are.

—*Jim Henson*

Acknowledgments

This book was a labor of love and I really want to thank the people who helped make it a reality.

Lisa Sharkey, Amy Bendell, Paige Hazzan, and the team at HarperCollins, thank you for having faith in me and believing in this project.

Brian Dow, thank you so much for your support in dealing with the craziness that has become my life.

And to Kevin Dickson, my partner in crime: we did it. I love you to death.